MAWDDACT  Y
TR

A long distance walk around the beautiful Mawddach
Estuary and the ancient upland and coastal areas of
Ardudwy, linking Barmouth, Dolgellau,
Porthmadog and Harlech

David Berry

KITTIWAKE

About the author

David is an experienced walker with a love of the countryside and an interest in local history. He is the author of many Kittiwake walks guidebooks covering North Wales, where he has lived and worked for many years. Whether on a riverside ramble or mountain walk he greatly appreciates the beauty, culture and history of the landscape and hopes that his comprehensive guidebooks will encourage people to explore on foot its diverse scenery and rich heritage.

He has undertaken many long distance walks, including coast to coast crossings of England, Scotland and Wales. He has used this experience to devise The Dee Way, a long distance cross border walk following the river Dee to its source in Southern Snowdonia. In 2012 he followed this up with The Conwy Valley Way, a long distance walk around the beautiful Conwy Valley from Conwy Bay to the river's source at Llyn Conwy.

He has worked as a Rights of Way surveyor across North Wales, been a freelance writer for Walking Wales magazine, and has served as a member of his Local Access Forum.

For more information visit www.davidberrywalks.co.uk

Acknowledgements

I wish to thank those people responsible for creating the Ardudwy Way, which inspired me to create this long distance trail. Also thanks to David Coleman at Gwynedd Council Rights of Way section for the advice and assistance given, and to David at Benar Beach Camping Park, near Tal-y-bont, for his hospitality and enthusiasm for promoting the area.

Published by Kittiwake Books Limited
3 Glantwymyn Village Workshops, Glantwymyn, Machynlleth, Montgomeryshire SY20 8LY

Printed by Mixam UK.

ISBN: 978 1 908748 10 2

Contents

Introduction

The Route

Linear walks   85

Guidance Notes & Useful Information

Descending towards the Mawddach estuary

INTRODUCTION

Arudwy and the Mawddach estuary

The western edge of Snowdonia National Park in Meirionnydd, lying between the Mawddach and Dwyryd estuaries, contains some of the most beautiful upland and coastal scenery in Wales, with breathtaking views. Most falls within the large ancient district of Ardudwy. The area offers a stunning diverse landscape of mountains, foothills, woodland, valleys, lakes, estuaries, impressive sand dunes and long sandy beaches. Its upland landscape is crossed by important ancient trackways and is renowned for its extensive archaeological remains, mainly late prehistoric. These include ancient hut settlements and field systems, Neolithic chambered tombs, Iron Age hillforts, Bronze Age stone circles and standing stones.

The ancient area of Ardudwy extended north from the northern side of the Mawddach estuary past Harlech to beyond the Afon Dwyryd and Vale of Ffestiniog. The Rhinog mountains and Trawsfynydd formed its main border in the east and the coast of Cardigan Bay its boundary in the west. Ardudwy, which formed part of the traditional Welsh Princes' heartland of Gwynedd, became absorbed into the new county of Merionethshire in 1284 after the English conquest of Wales, and is now part of modern Gwynedd. Through this largely upland area the glacial river valleys of the Artro, Cwmnantcol and Ysgethin head to a coastal plain that includes Morfa Dyffryn and Morfa Harlech National Nature Reserves. The coastal area is particularly popular with holidaymakers, with its sandy beaches and sand dunes, especially around Shell Island. Ardudwy includes several ancient churches and impressive Harlech castle, built for Edward I in the late 13thC to consolidate the Crown's control and power over North Wales. It is now a World Heritage Site.

The Mawddach estuary was carved into a 'U' shape during the last Ice Age over 10,000 years ago by a huge glacier and subsequently filled by silt. The estuary is now a Special Site of Scientific Interest because of its saltmarsh and lowland wet habitats. From the wooded edge of the estuary land rises south to the stunning Cregennan lakes, owned by the National Trust set beneath the impressive Cadair Idris range, and north to the foothills of the Rhinog mountains.

By the early 19thC the stunning beauty of the area was regularly attracting visitors and artists. Barmouth, with its long sandy beach and picturesque harbour, became established as a fashionable sea-side resort and people came to the historic market town of Dolgellau to climb Cadair Idris or go on excursions. The poet William Wordsworth's visit to Barmouth here in 1824 led him to describe the estuary as 'sublime'. John Ruskin, poet, painter and philanthropist said only one journey in the world had views to compare with the one from Dolgellau to Barmouth, and that was the journey from Barmouth to Dolgellau!

From the end of the 18thC travelling along the estuary was much improved with the building of turnpike roads from Dolgellau to Barmouth, then later along the south side of the estuary to Dolgellau. The arrival of the railway in 1867 was a great boost to the area, bringing in many more visitors and leading to the creation of new communities like Fairbourne. Wealthy industrialists from the Midlands were attracted to the area, building large country houses and adding new trees and gardens to the traditional native oak woodland.

It is hard to believe that to-day's tranquil estuary was once a hive of activity. Its creeks supported numerous shipyards attracted by the plentiful local oak, and between 1750–1865, 318 vessels were launched on the Mawddach. The estuary was navigable for boats under 20 tons to within 2 miles of Dolgellau. Barmouth became a flourishing seaport and small sailing boats travelled up and down the estuary, carrying various goods, most notably woollen 'webs' woven locally.

During the 19thC the area was exploited for its mineral wealth. In the hills on the northern side of the estuary there was limited mining of zinc, lead ore, manganese, silver and copper. However, in the middle of the 19thC the area above Bontddu was extensively mined for gold, and produced the famous Clogau gold used to make wedding rings for the Royal Family. Evidence of this remains to be seen in the landscape today in the form of mine entrances, upland tramways and old mill sites. On the southern side of the estuary the hillside at Friog was quarried for slate, and mined for silver, lead, manganese and copper. There was an additional slate quarry at nearby Arthog.

The Mawddach–Arudwy Trail

The Mawddach estuary and its surrounding hills is one of my favourite walking areas in North Wales and I have written a guidebook entitled 'Walks around Barmouth and the Mawddach estuary'. I was interested, therefore, to hear about the creation in 2010 of a promoted linear 24 mile upland walk called the Arudwy Way between Barmouth and Llandecwyn. It was developed as a tourism initiative by a local business group wishing to promote the Arudwy area, in conjunction with Gwynedd Council, Snowdonia National Park Authority, Countryside Council for Wales and was Lottery funded. I was familiar with the southern section, but the rest of the route was little known. In Spring 2011 I decided to camp at Tal-y-bont and walk the Arudwy Way in stages using the local bus. Most of my walking in recent years has been spent researching routes for new guidebooks or reviewing my existing routes for new editions. So the Arudwy Way offered me the opportunity to walk someone else's route for pleasure. And did I enjoy it! Although not great in length, the Arudwy Way is a superb well waymarked upland walk, following good paths and tracks through the relatively little known foothills of the Rhinogs, with great mountain and coastal views. Fortunately the weather was good which helped to enhance the scenic value of this remote treeless landscape.

Purely by chance at the end of the trip I got the opportunity to meet members of the business group and was able to provide feedback and compliment them on the standard of the walk. Their challenge was how to further promote the Way. Afterwards I wondered how I could help to make more people aware of this gem of a walk. I had previously devised two long distance walking routes – The Dee Way and the Conwy Valley Way – and saw the potential for another long distance trail. Kittiwake, which had published guidebooks on both these long distance routes was supportive of this idea. Early in 2012 I met with Gwynedd Council officers to seek advice on the concept of integrating the Arudwy Way with a route around the Mawddach Estuary, and the new Wales Coast Path that was currently under development for opening in May that year.

With Barmouth as a key starting and finishing point it was clearly feasible to create a long distance trail that first explored both sides of the stunning Mawddach estuary, then headed north on the Arudwy Way to Llandecwyn, where it linked with the new Coast Path. There were then two options: the

7

first was to follow the Coast Path back to Barmouth and the second to follow the Coast Path around the Dwyryd valley to finish at Porthmadog, which lies just outside the Ardudwy area. Until the building of a new road bridge with pathway across the Dwyryd in the next three years to replace the narrow old toll bridge, the Coast Path was having to take a circuitous route inland. This offered the opportunity of exploring the wooded Dwyryd valley, enjoying close encounters with steam trains on the narrow gauge Ffestiniog Railway, visiting famous Portmeirion, and a walk across the Cob to the former slate port. From Porthmadog, a short train journey returned you to Llandecwyn to join the Coast Path on its journey back to Barmouth.

One of the wettest summers on record frustrated my planned research of the route, but eventually all sections of the trail fell into place.

The trail that I have devised offers:

– a continuous long distance trail of up to 94 miles exploring both sides of the Mawddach estuary, the foothills of the Rhinogs, the lower Dwyryd valley to Porthmadog, then returning along the coast to Barmouth, with a choice of routes on some sections.

– a route that incorporates diverse landscape features, classic viewpoints, historic towns and villages, ancient highways, prehistoric monuments and other sites of historical interest.

– a route that links four popular tourist destinations - Barmouth, Dolgellau, Porthmadog and Harlech.

– a start (Barmouth) and finish (either Barmouth or Porthmadog) linked to the National Rail Network to facilitate easy access from and departure to anywhere in Britain.

– a route that can be tailored to individual requirements.

– opportunities for multi-day walks and day/half day walks of variable lengths. A key feature of the trail is that it is supported by easily accessible public transport throughout its length, allowing each section to be undertaken as linear day walks. I have broken the trail down into 14 linear walks linked to local transport, which can easily be combined with others to provide longer day walks if necessary.

– a fascinating insight into the history of the area and the various communities that the trail passes through.

The trail follows public rights of way, permissive paths and crosses Open Access land. It uses paths, bridleways, tracks, scenic minor roads and beach walking. It falls within the Meirionnydd district of Gwynedd Council.

The new trail will appeal to people of all ages and abilities, from experienced walkers who enjoy the challenge of completing a continuous walking trail, to people who want to learn more about the area's rich heritage through shorter day walks.

Overview of the trail

From Barmouth the Mawddach-Ardudwy trail crosses the famous Victorian Barmouth Bridge to begin an exploration of the southern side of the beautiful Mawddach estuary. One option is to continue along the low level Mawddach Trail to Dolgellau. The main trail however takes a more undulating approach to Dolgellau, exploring the stunning landscape of foothills and valleys beneath the Cadair Idris mountain range. The route rises from Arthog Bog past waterfalls and ancient sites to the beautiful Cregennan Lakes set in a wide upland valley, then continues east to Kings Youth Hostel situated in the wooded Gwynant valley. From here there is a choice of equally attractive routes to Dolgellau, either by Penmaenpool and the Mawddach Trail, or by Llyn Gwernan.

The trail returns to Barmouth along the northern side of the Mawddach estuary following an undulating route through a beautiful varied and historic landscape of foothills, narrow wooded river valleys, woodland and the estuary itself. It passes through an area near Bontddu famous for its gold-mining and Coedgarth-Gell Nature Reserve. It visits ruined Cymer Abbey, follows ancient highways and includes one of the area's highlights – the New Precipice Walk, offering stunning views. The final section from Sylfaen has a choice of high and low routes, the latter including another classic viewpoint – the Panorama Walk, popular since Victorian times. Also included is an alternative high level direct route from Coedgarth-Gell Nature Reserve to Pont Hirgwm, which maintains height and by-passes Bontddu.

From Barmouth the trail now joins the waymarked Ardudwy Way as it begins its journey north through the former medieval administrative area of Ardudwy, crossing some of the oldest rock strata in Wales, known as the Harlech Dome. It first crosses a fascinating upland area, important since prehistoric times, featuring two ancient mountain passes and highways, Bronze Age monuments and extensive views. It passes a described link route down to Tal-y-bont then continues along remote Cwm Ysgethin past Llyn Erddyn to the ancient stone bridge of Pont Scethin. It continues along

The old Harlech coach road

a section of an ancient upland highway, passing beneath Moelfre, then heads across country to a minor road, which offers a link down to Dyffryn Ardudwy. From nearby Ffynnon Enddwyn, an ancient healing well, the trail continues north down into Cwm Nantcol, then leaves the Ardudwy Way to descend to Llanbedr.

The trail then heads back past famous Capel Salem to rejoin the Ardudwy Way and continues north to a small attractive lake, then rises across a hidden upland area to a minor upland road, which offers a link down to either Llanfair or Harlech. The trail continues northwards with the Ardudwy Way through a wild ancient upland landscape to the stunning Bronze Age burial site of Bryn Cader Faner, beneath the northern end of the Rhinog ridge. It then begins a long steady descent to Llyn Tecwyn Isaf, from where there are a choice of routes down to Llandecwyn and the end of the Ardudwy Way. From here you can follow the Coast Path back to Barmouth. The main trail follows the Coast Path around the wooded Cwm Dwyryd to Penrhyndeudraeth then continues via Portmeirion to Porthmadog, with the narrow gauge Ffestiniog Railway featuring strongly.

After returning by train to Llandecwyn the trail follows the Coast Path to Harlech then via Shell Island and Tal-y-bont to finish at the harbour in Barmouth. This section features several ancient churches and a coastal landscape of saltmarsh edges, creeks, estuaries, impressive sand dunes and beautiful sandy beaches.

BARMOUTH TO DOLGELLAU
9¾, 12¼ or 13¼ miles

After crossing the famous railway viaduct to the southern side of the Mawddach estuary the trail heads eastwards to Dolgellau. The easiest and shortest option is to follow the Mawddach Trail, a popular level recreational route along the edge of the estuary for walkers and cyclists, mainly using the trackbed of the former Ruabon-Barmouth railway line. This is described on pages 26-27. However the main trail leaves the estuary to explore the stunning upland landscape beneath the Cadair Idris range, before following a choice of routes to Dolgellau.

1 Barmouth to Snowdonia National Park Arthog car park
3½ miles

The first section of the trail follows the promenade round to the harbour for classic views, visits the town's 19thC 'lock-up', then continues to one of the trail's highlights – a walk over the iconic 19thC railway viaduct across the the mouth of the Mawddach estuary, offering stunning views. A small toll is payable to use the walkway alongside the railway track. After a short section of the Mawddach Trail it follows a bridleway through Arthog Bog to the edge of the estuary for good views, then continues by path and minor road back to rejoin the Mawddach Trail at the site of the former Arthog station, now a small car park.

Barmouth

Barmouth stands at the mouth of the Mawddach estuary where the river enters Cardigan Bay and at a key ferry crossing point. Although the nearby hills and upland valleys contain extensive evidence of the presence of man here in prehistoric times, the origin of Barmouth is more recent and maritime in nature. It was first recorded as a small fishing settlement in the 16thC, but It developed over the next two centuries as the commercial port for the Mawddach area, including Dolgellau. By the end of the 18thC it was a thriving small port, with about 100 registered ships engaging in coastal and continental trading, including Ireland, Spain and Italy, based mainly on the county's woollen industry. Its original Welsh name of Aber Maw (mouth of the river Maw) was anglicised in 1768 at a meeting of masters of vessels belonging to the port. With a growing population rows of cottages were built on the steep rocky slopes of the hill overlooking the town. In 1842 it was written that 'the appearance of the town, as viewed from the sea, is peculiarly romantic: the houses, rising in successive tiers from the base nearly to the summit.' Now known as Old Barmouth these old dwellings accessed by narrow lanes remain a feature of the town.

The growth in trade necessitated

the enlargement of the harbour and the building of a new quay in 1802, which increased the depth of water, allowing the port to continue to flourish during the first half of the 19thC. Exports from the Mawddach included timber, pit props for collieries, oak bark (used for tanning leather), woollen 'webs' – a coarse white cloth woven in the area, manganese, copper, lead ore and for a brief period slate from small quarries along the estuary. Imports included limestone, coal from South Wales, corn, flour, meal, sugar, soap and candles.

By the early 19thC Barmouth had also become an important ship building centre, with many small shipyards operating along the estuary, producing magnificent square riggers. At the same time it was also emerging as a fashionable sea-bathing resort, with the area's stunning scenery also attracting famous travellers and writers, such as Thomas Pennant, William Wordsworth, Shelley, Charles Darwin, and John Ruskin, as well as artists. The town offered a fine hotel and numerous boarding houses for visitors,along with warm and cold sea-water baths. The increasing number of vessels heading along the exposed coast to Barmouth faced possible shipwreck in stormy weather, and so a lifeboat station was established here in 1828. It has provided continuous service ever since.

The arrival of the railway in 1867 after the building of the railway viaduct, whilst precipitating the decline in the importance of the port, the shipping industry and its seafaring tradition, brought in many more visitors, drawn by sand, sea, the curative powers of scurvy grass, and the mountainous hinterland. Many travelled by train along the Mawddach estuary on the Ruabon-Barmouth line from various parts of the country. Barmouth rapidly developed into an important late Victorian sea-side resort, with a large part of the town you see today dating from that period. Its importance as a resort continued into the 20thC, with a reported 1600 day visitors arriving in Barmouth by rail in 1920. Although its heyday has long since passed the town still remains a popular holiday destination and is proud of its long maritime history.

From the Railway Station turn right and at the junction right again to cross the railway. Continue along the road to join the palm tree lined promenade. Follow it south past the extensive beach. *You pass a sea wall extending to nearby Ynys y Brawd, originally a small island and now an area of sand dunes after being linked to the mainland as part of a sea flood defence.* Go past The Bath House and on to reach the dolphin water feature *– with a good view across the mouth of the estuary.* Follow the signposted Coast Path above the harbour, past the nearby Lifeboat Museum, toilets and the ferry crossing point to Fairbourne Railway.

From at least medieval times a ferry has carried people across the mouth of the estuary. Once it was run by local monks from Ynys y Brawd. After the Reformation it was run by local fishermen. In the 19thC, it was owned by the Barmouth Harbour Trust, and operated by tenants of Penrhyn Farm on Porth Penrhyn opposite until it was sold in 1860. There were two boats, one for passengers, and the other for animals, wheeled vehicles and general goods. It also an important link in the Royal Mail route which ran from Dolgellau along the northern side of the estuary to Barmouth, first by a 17thC road then the turnpike road, now the A496, before heading south along the coast to Tywyn and on to Machynlleth. Inevitably, traffic greatly decreased with the arrival of the railway in 1867. In the 20thC, the ferrymen came to rely upon the Fairbourne narrow gauge railway for a living and it still carries visitors today across to its terminus.

Now go up the short road past the side of Ty Gwyn. *One of the oldest buildings in Barmouth, dating from 1460, it is now now used as Davey Jones Locker cafe and contains a small museum displaying artefacts from the 'Bronze Bell' shipwreck.* Continue up to Ty Trwn Roundhouse – *a lock-up used between 1834-1861 for petty offenders, drunkards and detainees awaiting transfer to court. This small simple stone structure contained two cells, one for men, one for women. Nearby is an information board on Ty Gwyn.* Return to continue along the harbour enjoying breathtaking views across the water to the railway viaduct and Cadair Idris beyond. *Nearby is the Sailor's Institute built in 1890 to provide a reading and* meeting room for the town's mariners. *It now contains interesting artefacts depicting the town's maritime history.* Pass under the railway bridge. *On the harbour-side is an unusual modern sculpture carved by a local artist out of a block of Italian marble retrieved from an early 18thC 'Bronze Bell' 'shipwreck found just off the coast in 1978. It represents three generations of fishermen pulling in their catch.* Turn right along the shoreline edge of a small garden area beneath the railway, passing a cannon and an anchor. Cross the road and continue along the pavement opposite out of Barmouth, soon rising. When it levels out by large crags covered in steel mesh cross the road with care to go through a waymarked gap in the wall opposite into a small garden area – *offering good views back to the harbour, across the mouth of the estuary towards Fairbourne and hills beyond, and across the viaduct to Cadair Idris.* Turn left along its edge past a shelter to go through another wall gap. Turn

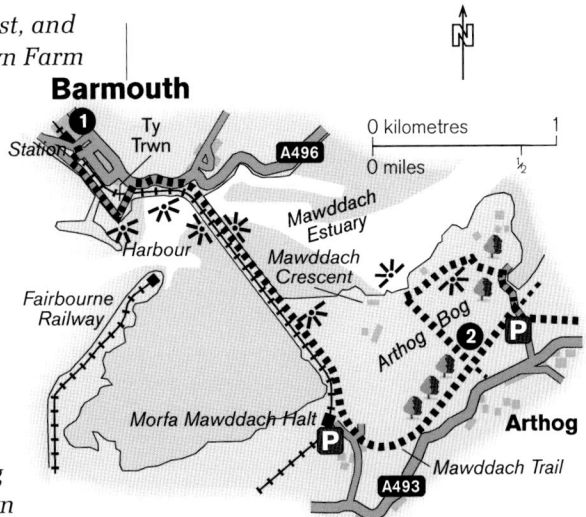

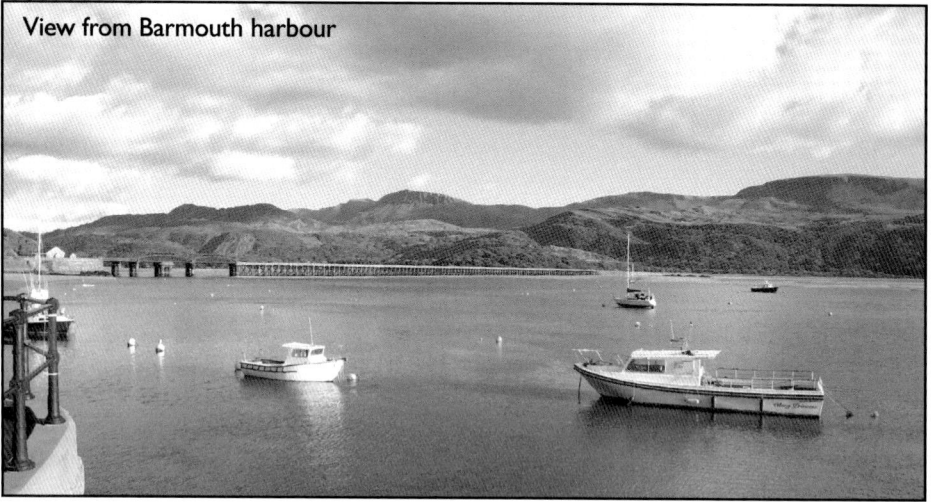

View from Barmouth harbour

right along the road edge a few yards beneath the start of Porkington Terrace – *a row of large four storey terraced houses built in 1870* – then descend the wide pathway and continue beside the railway to the Barmouth bridge toll booth.

The railway viaduct stretching for ½ mile across the mouth of the estuary is a great feat of Victorian engineering and one of the wonders of Wales. It provided an essential section of the new coastal railway linking Aberystwyth with Pwllheli. Building the wooden bridge, consisting of 113 spans supported by over 500 timber piles, was challenging due to strong currents, but it eventually opened in 1867. For a few months as the bridge was nearing completion, passengers were taken over the bridge in a carriage drawn by two horses. This must have been quite a sight! The railway gave local people access to various parts of Britain, and brought in many middle class Victorian visitors. It boosted the development of Barmouth

and led to the creation of Fairbourne. Its original wooden lifting drawbridge over the navigation channel to allow the passage of tall ships, was replaced in 1899 by the current steel swing bridge, which requires eight men to operate manually. It is some time since it was used. Thankfully the bridge has survived closure threats, notably in 1980 from damage to the wooden timbers caused by the teredo worm, and regular locomotive-hauled trains continue to cross this historic structure.

After paying the small toll walk across the bridge alongside the railway – *enjoying extensive estuary and mountain views and if timed right the experience of a close encounter with a passing train.* At the estuary's mouth can be seen the terminus of the Fairbourne Railway. *The famous 2½ mile narrow gauge steam railway originates from a 2 ft gauge horse drawn tramway built by Arthur McDougal (of flour fame) in 1895, initially for transporting materials*

Barmouth viaduct

for the building of Fairbourne, but extended to the ferry between 1897-98 and used to carry summer visitors. *In 1916 the tramway was sold and converted into a miniature steam railway, which opened in 1919. Since then it has had a chequered history, experiencing many changes of ownership, periods of prosperity and decay, and severe flooding damage. But it has survived into the 21stC and continues to delight passengers today as the original tramway did in the late 1890s!*

At the other side of the bridge continue with the wide surfaced recreational route alongside the railway – *with a view ahead of the hills above Friog and the old slate quarries.* You cross a stream and pass a signposted path. *Near the next small gate on the left, just before Morfa Mawddach halt, once stood a refreshment and waiting room built in 1899 at the start of a horse-drawn tramway – still visible. Both were part of ambitious plans by Solomon*

Andrews, a remarkable self-made businessman, to develop the nearby area into a resort as he had at Pwllheli. The tramway took visitors to the estuary, then in 1903, on a circuit of Fegla Fawr, passing the three storey Mawddach Crescent he had built. After then his plans came to an end. Continue with the Mawddach Trail past Morfa Mawddach halt, which was originally called Barmouth Junction. *In 1868 a siding was added here to take slate brought down from the quarries above Ffriog. In 1869 it connected with a standard gauge railway line developed in stages from Ruabon via Llangollen and Dolgellau.* Continue past the adjoining car park then toilets. The Trail continues through trees and crosses a road to gates opposite.

Nearby is the small holiday village of Fairbourne built by Arthur McDougal. In 1895, he purchased land, with the intention of creating an elite sea-side resort to be called South Barmouth. His ambitious plans, which included a pier, were never fully realised by the time he sold the estate in 1912, being unable to compete with the better facilities of Barmouth. The village takes its name from the new railway station he had built in 1899.

The Trail now begins its journey eastwards along the tree-lined trackbed of the former Ruabon-Barmouth railway.

Apart from briefly carrying slate from the Ty'n y Coed quarry at Arthog, the main role of the branch line became to bring countless visitors into the area, including many from London. Even as late as the 1950s, despite the increased competition from cars, there were 5 through trains each weekday, plus local trains from Dolgellau to Barmouth. On summer Saturdays trains from different parts of England full of passengers, many bound for Butlins in Pwllheli, passed this way. Sadly, the highly scenic line closed in 1965 – a victim of the infamous Beeching cuts in the National Rail Network.

Shortly the Trail passes a path on the right leading to Arthog Bog RSPB Nature Reserve, then crosses a small bridge before continuing through trees. *Arthog Bog, known locally as Y Fawnog, contains many uncommon grasses and plants, attracting birds and butterflies. In the 19thC peat was dug up and taken away in sailing boats to be used as fuel.* As the trees begin to thin out the Trail is crossed by a bridleway.

2 Here you have a choice. You can simply continue along the Mawddach Trail to a minor road by the Snowdonia National Park Authority Arthog car park on the site of the former Arthog Station. My preferred route turns left to the nearby gate, then follows the bridleway past woodland to an iron gate and across Arthog Bog to reach two adjoining small gates at the edge of the estuary near Fegla Fawr. *Here are views to the railway viaduct and directly across the estuary to a low hill containing the Panorama Walk, and a transmitter mast beneath the higher mountain ridge that feature on the later final routes to Barmouth. If you turn left along the track by the estuary you will have a view of nearby Mawddach Crescent built by Solomon Andrews referred to earlier. From 1941 during the Second World War the Royal Marines ran a training camp on nearby Fegla Fawr, code named Iceland, and the bases of their huts can still be seen in the wood.* Go through the gate on the right and along the signposted path, soon joining the access track to Bryn Celyn Lodge amongst trees. When it bends left after a few yards, continue ahead on the signposted path along the edge of Arthog Bog – *with good views across to the Cadair Idris mountain range.* The path passes a finger post and continues along the edge of reedy ground to a small gate by another finger post just below an access lane to Tyddyn Uchaf. The path continues through an area of small trees to reach Fegla Fach farm's access road. Follow it right to rejoin the Mawddach Trail, by the small Snowdonia National Park Arthog car park.

2 Snowdonia National Park Arthog car park to Kings Youth Hostel

4¼ miles

The next section follows a riverside path to St Catherine's Church in Arthog – a small roadside estate village that developed during the 19thC following the opening of the railway. It then rises through a narrow wooded valley past Arthog Falls to cross a delightful stone clapper bridge. The trail continues across enclosed upland pasture past an ancient stone circle, to the stunningly beautiful Cregennan Lakes, owned by the National Trust, set in a wide hidden upland valley beneath the Cadair Idris range, an important area since prehistoric times. After exploring the two lakes, using available National Trust waymarked paths, the trail heads east along the edge of the treeless valley. It then descends into a narrow wooded side valley containing a remote ruined chapel, before making a final descent through attractive woodland to Kings youth hostel situated in the wooded Gwynant valley.

1 Continue along the road by a small inlet – *with the castellated 19thC Arthog Hall, built by a Lancashire cotton mill owner, prominent on the wooded hillside and further east the remains of the Ty'n y Coed slate quarry which opened in 1860.* Shortly cross a ladder-stile on the left and follow the signposted path, soon alongside the Afon Arthog, to reach the A493 near St Catherine's Church. Cross the road and turn left, then take a signposted path through a small iron gate opposite the church entrance. Follow the path up the edge of the wooded side valley above the river. After passing old stone gateposts go along the wide path ahead, then take a narrower waymarked path on the right up through trees. The path rises steadily alongside the river cascading down a narrow rocky gorge. Just before Arthog lower falls, the path bends sharply away from the river and meanders up the wooded slope, then continues to a ladder-stile in a wall. The stiled path now rises up the edge of the wooded valley past further falls to a ladder-stile at the top to emerge from the trees – *with a view of the distinctive crag of Craig-las.*

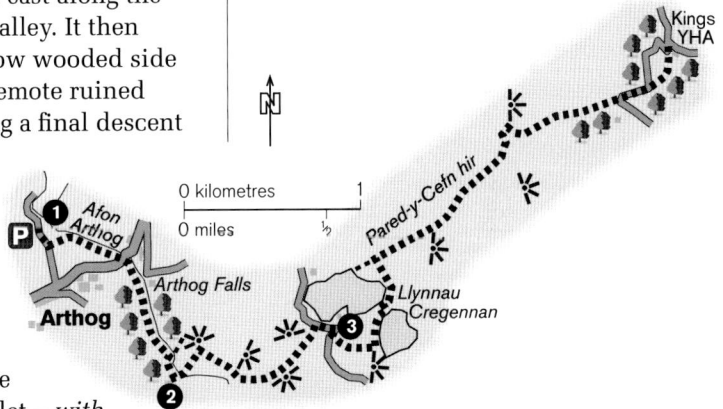

2 At a green track just beyond turn left to cross a delightful nearby stone clapper bridge over the river. *On the riverbank just upstream is the site of two adjoining medieval buildings, known as Llys Bradwen, reputed to have been the court of Bradwen, leader*

of one of the 15 tribes of North Wales in the early 12thC. The path rises to join a nearby track, which you follow to a gate – *enjoying extensive views across the estuary towards Diffwys and the Llawlach ridge, then Barmouth.* Continue along the stony track, past another track leading down left – *with a panoramic view down to the railway viaduct at the mouth of the estuary, Barmouth and the distant Llyn peninsula.* Keep ahead up the track to go through another gate. Ignore the waymarked path ahead but turn right and follow a track along the field edge to a gate. Go ahead along the next field edge to another gate – *enjoying a good view ahead of the craggy top of Craig-las on the Cadair Idris range, and into the wild upland valley beyond a large farmhouse nestling below.* Continue beside the wall through the next large field – *past the remains of an ancient stone circle in the adjoining field.* At gates in the wall corner turn left and follow the signposted path up near the wall, soon being joined by another wall on the left. Go through the facing gate then turn left on the path alongside the wall, soon angling right away from it, and continuing up across upland pasture. The path then levels out – *with the distinctive rocky ridge of Pared y Cefn-hir visible ahead.* The wide path now descends and joins the wall on the left to reach a stone stile in the corner. Just beyond, the path bends half-left and rises gently past a path on the right to a view of the first Cregennan lake beneath Pared y Cefn-hir, then continues to a minor road above the lake. Turn right along the road past Scots pines, soon bending left, then right up to a gate across the road, with a nearby house ahead.

3 Just beyond the gate turn left up a path by the wall for a few yards then angle right to pass the wall corner ahead. Continue east beside the wall, soon descending to cross a ladder-stile over it by a boathouse on the second lake. *The lakes carry the name of a medieval township in the area. Cairns and standing stones just to the south indicates that the Cregennan area has been used by man for burial and ritual purposes since the second millennium BC. It is linked to two ancient routes – Ffordd Ddu and another prehistoric route from the west. Ffordd Ddu (Black Road), part of which is now the minor road running beneath the Cadair Idris range, is an ancient mountain route running from Dolgellau to Llanegryn, where it connected with others that led to the Upper Severn valley and England. In this area it had branches down to Arthog, Friog and Llwyngwril. It is believed to be part of the Roman Road network linking West Wales with garrisons at Chester and near Shrewsbury, a route serving smaller camps near the coast. During the Middle Ages it became an important route for local Welsh gentry seeking patronage with London and the Royal Court. It also attracted bandits, especially the notorious 'Red Men of Dinas Mawddwy'. It was used regularly as a coach road until the building of the Turnpike coastal road in the 19thC.*
Follow a waymarked National Trust path along the side of the lake, soon bending away from its corner to cross a stile in the wall on the

Cregennan lake and Craig-las

right near the first lake, then a stream and ladder-stile beyond. Follow the path alongside the lake, crossing a footbridge over the lake's outlet stream. Soon afterwards the path rises gently ahead and continues across open ground to a small waymark post at a wide cross path beneath Pared y Cefn-hir. *On this exposed rocky volcanic ridge are the remains of a small Iron Age hillfort.* Turn right and follow the path along the edge of the wild upland valley – *now with a good view of Cadair Idris* – shortly accompanied by a wall on your right and enjoying new views east to the distant Arans. Eventually the path bends left with the wall, then descends, with a large house below, to a ladder-stile/gate. Angle right down to a gateway in the

wall, then follow the waymarked path down a faint green track to another old gateway in a wall and on near a low wall on your right – *enjoying a great view of the majestic Cadair Idris ridge.* The track becomes more distinct and steadily descends to a gate above the river, which it then follows down to a minor road. Go along the road ahead and down above the attractive narrow wooded river valley to a small ruined chapel and neat graveyard, still used today. Here take a wide signposted path on the right down through attractive woodland to a stream and a small gate to join a minor road beyond. Follow it down to a junction by Kings Youth Hostel in the wooded Gwynant valley.

3 Kings Youth Hostel to Eldon Square, Dolgellau
4½ or 5½ miles

There is now a choice of interesting routes to Dolgellau:

Route A (5½ miles) is an undulating route of great variety, featuring one of the Mawddach estuary's highlights - an opportunity to enjoy refreshments sitting outside the George III Hotel overlooking the river by the old toll bridge at Penmaenpool. After following the narrow road down the attractive wooded Gwynant valley to a former school, now a bunkhouse, the route follows a delightful green track, offering breathtaking mountain and estuary views, up to an area of small shapely peaks. A path then descends across enclosed upland pasture and through woodland to Penmaenpool. Here it joins the Mawddach Trail for a steady walk through Penmaenpool Reeds, a Site of Special Scientific Interest, to Pont-y-Wernddu, followed by a final riverside section to Dolgellau.

Route B (4½ miles) takes a shorter more direct approach to Dolgellau offering closer views of Cadair Idris. It first follows tracks, path, bridleway and a new waymarked courtesy path agreed between the landowner and Snowdonia National Park Authority (closed February 5th every year) to attractive Llyn Gwernan, a popular fishing lake. It then continues to a scenic upland road, before following a delightful bridleway down to Dolgellau.

20

Route C (5½ miles) follows the river down the attractive wooded Gwynant valley to the A493, then past Abergwynant Farm to where it joins the Mawddach estuary. It then follows the Mawddach Trail to Penmaenpool, with its toll bridge, RSPB hide and the delightful George III Hotel, before continuing with Route A to Dolgellau.

Route A *(5½ miles)*
Kings to Penmaenpool *(3 miles)*

From Kings follow the narrow road down the wooded Gwynant valley, shortly crossing the river. Just before the entrance to Caban Cader Idris bunkhouse as the road begins to descend, turn right on a signposted path up Cae'n -y-Coed's rough access lane past the former school. Just beyond a gate when the stony track bends left towards Cae'n -y-Coed keep ahead up a green track to a ladder-stile near a gate. The delightful green track now meanders up the hillside - *with a good view across to the Cadair Idris ridge* – shortly being joined by a wall on the left – *with a good view back to Pared y Cefn-hir and distant Barmouth.* After a ladder-stile/gate continue up the track beneath knobbly peaks – *shortly with a good view north to Diffwys and the Rhinogs beyond, then Rhobell Fawr and Duallt further east.* As the track briefly levels out pause to look back at a breathtaking view of mountains and the Mawddach estuary. A little further turn left off the track to cross a stone stile in the nearby wall. Continue ahead and go up a wide green gap in the slope ahead on Dolgledr – *enjoying a view to Cadair*

Idris and eastwards down towards Dolgellau and distant mountains. Dolgledr is the name of a recorded medieval township in this area. Nearby is the peak of Craig y Castell on which is an ancient hillfort. From a post follow a wide path ahead down into upland pasture beneath a slope of large boulders, then follow a fence on your right down to a ladder-stile/gate. Go down the right-hand edge of the next field, then after going through a wide gap in an old wall bend right with a green track to cross a stream and ladder-stile. Continue along the track – *enjoying new views* – soon descending.

2 At a stone barn turn left down the field to a boundary corner below by trees and follow the wall down past a gate to go through a waymarked gate at its corner between outbuildings. Continue ahead towards the house then bend left on the waymarked path to another gate and follow the green track to a ladder-stile/gate. Continue along the track, shortly bending left to a ladder-stile. A little further, just before the track meets an old wall leading to a stone barn ahead, ignore the waymarked Tir Cymen path and turn right down the field past woodland and parallel with the wall on your right. Near the bottom follow the waymarked path to a small wooden gate in the left-hand corner. Keep ahead past the right-hand end of Gwern Barcud cottage to a large gate beyond. Continue down a green track, being joined by the one you left earlier. When the track bends right take the waymarked path ahead down through trees to a stile. Follow the path down through the wood to a stony track by a pond. Follow the track left down through woodland, soon joining another access track. Shortly, take a signposted path through a small iron gate on the right down past the end of a house then bending beneath it and descending to the A493 at Penmaenpool. Turn right with care along the road past the rear of the George III Hotel, with the toll bridge below, then cross to the other side and turn left down past the Hotel's entrance onto the former railway line above the estuary. *A popular bar with outside seats makes a delightful place to stop to enjoy good food and/or a drink.*

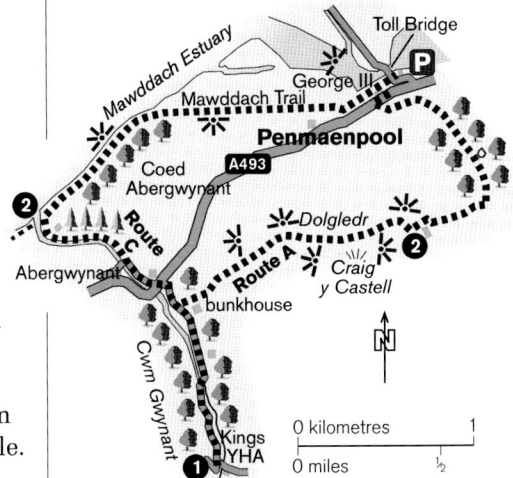

Penmaenpool to Eldon Square, Dolgellau *(2½ miles)*

At the beginning of the 19th C Penmaenpool, at a main bend of the river and a key ferry crossing point, had become one of the Mawddach's principal shipbuilding areas. Two-masted schooners were built here from local oak, before being towed to Barmouth by rowing boats for rigging and fitting of masts. Shipbuilding had more or less ceased with the arrival of the railway in 1867. Penmaenpool was built in the mid-19thC on the former turnpike road, now the A493, as an estate village for nearby Penmaenuchaf Hall, then owned by a mill owner from Bolton.

The George III Hotel, dating from 1650, was originally two buildings – one a pub and the other a ship's chandlers, serving the shipbuilding yard outside. It is said that the pub played an active role in smuggling, which was prevalent on the Mawddach. The buildings became the present hotel about 1890. The Hotel annexe was originally the former Victorian waiting room, ticket office and stationmaster's house for the station here, until the line was closed in 1964.

The timber toll bridge was built across the river in 1879 by the Penmaenpool Bridge Company to replace the ferry, becoming the lowest road crossing point of the Afon Mawddach. It connects the A493 to the A496 on the northern side of the estuary and originally offered a shorter journey around the estuary than having to go via Dolgellau. Sadly, in 1966 it was the scene of a tragedy when the Prince of Wales pleasure boat from Barmouth

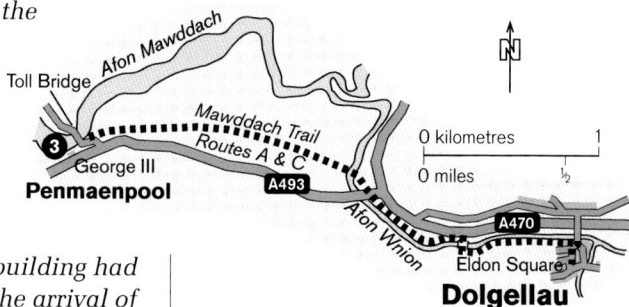

hit the bridge whilst attempting to tie up alongside the George III, throwing all passengers into the river and 15 people, including 4 children, died. The bridge, keeper's cottage, store and a strip of road was on sale for £350,000 as this book went to press.

3 From the George III cross the road by the entrance to the toll bridge. Go past the former signal box, now an RSPB information centre and bird hide, then toilets, and through the car park, built on the site of the former railway station. Continue east along the tree-lined Mawddach Trail adjoining the Penmaenpool reed bed – one of the largest areas of common reed in Wales and an important breeding area for wetland birds and otters. Through trees you can see on the northern side of the valley above the tree line the mine-scarred hill of Foel Ispri. Running across it is the line of an old tramway, now the New Precipice Walk – a highlight of the first section of the trail returning to Barmouth. Later the trail crosses Pont-y-Wernddu over the Afon Wnion, near where it joins the Afon Mawddach, into a small car park, marking the end of the former railway trackbed. At the road turn right then cross to the opposite side to follow the surfaced Mawddach Trail alongside the Afon Wnion, shortly crossing to the opposite bank, and continuing beside the river – *with a good view of Cadair Idris – past a large recreational area, known as 'The Marian', given in trust to the town to facilitate various leisure activities. It contains a stone circle built to mark the National Eisteddfod of Wales being here in 1949.* When you reach the main car park in Dolgellau follow its riverside edge to reach the road by the bridge. Turn right, then follow the right fork (no through road) to Eldon Square.

Route B *(4½ miles)*

| Turn ight along the narrow road signposted to 'Hafod Dywyll camping' past the youth hostel and over the river to the campsite entrance. Continue up the road, past Hafod Olau on the left to a gate, then go up the rough lane ahead. After passing outbuildings bend right up a stony track to a gate above the large old 17thC stone house. Continue up the stony track and when it does a U-turn left keep ahead on a waymarked path along a green track to a ladder-stile/gate. Continue up the track – *soon with a good view ahead to the crags of Cadair Idris* – then just after it bends left go through a small waymarked gate down to your right. Follow the path down through trees and on to a small gate. Cross the stream beyond and follow the path up to a waymarked bridleway/path junction. Turn left up the bridleway, soon accompanied by a wall on your left to pass a small ruined dwelling. The waymarked bridleway then rises up a slope, after a few yards bending right, to a gate in the wall – *with a good view looking back to Diffwys.* Continue between an old wall and a fence then along a field edge down to a gate and on to another gate at Tyddyn-Evan-fychan. Go ahead past outbuildings and the house, then down the farm's access track – *which offers a good appreciation of the grandeur of Cadair Idris, now so close and towering above the part wooded valley.* Go over a cattle grid just beyond a side track leading to Owen Tyddyn farm, and continue along the stony track past a house.

2 Just before the road crosses the river, with a car park beyond used as the starting point for a climb up Cadair Idris, turn sharp left along the access drive to Thomas. After a few yards turn right and follow a waymarked path past a solitary tree to a waymarked path junction. Take the waymarked white courtesy path to a ladder stile. The path now follows the boundary on your left past a wet reedy area. At its corner go to a waymark post ahead and turn left with the courtesy path, over the remains of an old wall and on to a finger post. Turn right and follow the waymarked path by an old wall, through a wall gap and on to a ladder-stile/gate. The waymarked courtesy path continues through conifers to a ladder-stile, then through deciduous trees and a gap in the wall. *Here a boardwalked path leads right to the nearby road by Gwernan Hotel, a former gentlemen's shooting lodge, if you seek* *refreshments (limited opening hours Thurs/Fri/Sat only).* The trail follows the path ahead through tall Scots pines to a small gate, then continues along the wooded edge of attractive Gwernan lake and passes through a wall gap. At a waymarked path junction by a large Private Fishing board the trail continues with the public footpath. But first follow the courtesy path near the lake to a seat offering a good view of the lake and the Cadair Idris range beyond. *The natural lake, 12 acres in size contains a variety of fish, including perch, trout, sea trout and eels, and is popular for fishing. Its edges also provides a habitat for various birds, dragonflies and damselflies. The boardwalked path, created by Snowdonia National Park Authority, passes through a Site of Special Scientific Interest due to the 12 metres of peat found here, containing a record of pollen from plants grown here since the last Ice Age, 10,000 years ago.*

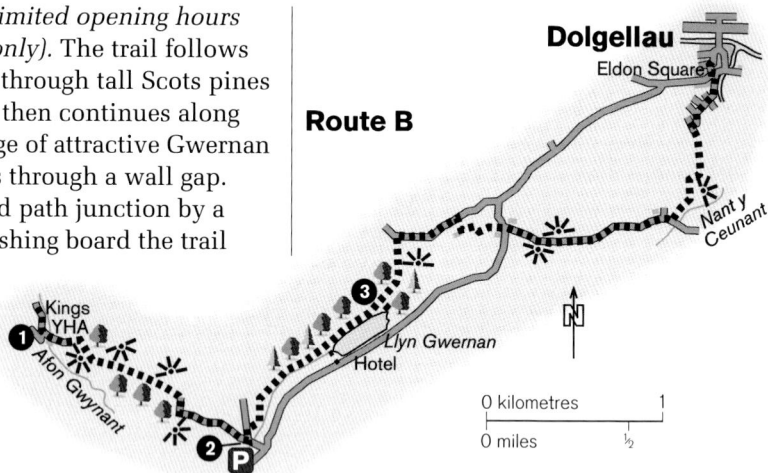

3 Return to the waymarked path junction and continue east on the waymarked public path through woodland to a ladder-stile at its edge. Follow the stony track ahead, shortly passing an old ruin, to join a minor road. Follow it right, soon descending. Shortly take a signposted path through a gate set back on the right and follow the track to the nearby house. Bear left past the house to the door at its end and through a small iron gate directly opposite. Cross the stream and walk beside the perimeter fence of woodland at the bottom of the sloping field. At the fence corner turn left on a wide stony path across the stream, through a gate and on between a fence and a wall. When the wall bends right keep ahead to cross another stream, then bear right up the field above the stream to a slate stile onto a road. Turn right then at the nearby road junction by Rhydwen turn left (signposted cycle route 21). Follow the scenic narrow upland road – *offering views of the lower wooded slopes of Cadair Idris and mountain ranges to the north* – later descending to a gate. Continue down the road past the entrance to Pentacota. Just before the road crosses the Nant y Ceunant take the signposted bridleway through a small gate on the left. Go along a stony track above the stream, shortly bending away from it and rising to a good viewpoint, where the track ends. Keep ahead with the green bridleway, descending in stages.

Llyn Gwernan

Just before a facing wall the bridleway bends down right then goes through an iron gate in the wall in the old field corner. Follow the enclosed tree-lined bridleway down the hillside – *with Dolgellau visible below.* Shortly It bends left past a finger post where a footpath joins and descends to a road by Y Bwthyn. Here turn right down a rough narrow lane, bending left past a seat to join a path which descends to the bend of a narrow road by Penybryn. Go down the road into Dolgellau past roads on the left. At crossroads keep ahead down Meyrick Street to reach Eldon Square in the heart of Dolgellau.

Route C *(5½ miles)*
See map on page 21.

I From Kings follow the narrow road down the wooded Gwynant valley, shortly crossing the river, to eventually reach the A493. Turn left for a few yards then go down Abergwynant Farm's driveway through mature trees near the river and past Ty Gwyn. When the road bends left across a bridge to Abergwynant Farm continue along the road ahead beside the river. When it bends right towards a house go through the waymarked metal gate ahead by the river. Go along a green track, taking its right fork to another gate. Bend left along the stony track, soon passing through trees above the river, and continuing near the river to join the Mawddach Trail at an old railway bridge over it.

2 Follow the Mawddach Trail east along the edge of the estuary past Coed Abergwynant. *One of only two surviving ancient native woodlands on this side of the estuary, it is owned and managed by Snowdonia National Park Authority. Conifers planted here during the 1960s have been removed and work undertaken to restore native sessile oak, birch and holly.* Shortly it bends away from the estuary and heads directly east along a straight section of the former railway to reach the George III Hotel at Penmaenpool. Continue along the Mawddach Trail to Dolgellau, following instructions in paragraph 3 of Route A. on pages 22-23.

Barmouth to Dolgellau via the Mawddach Trail
9¾, miles

The Mawddach Trail is a popular level recreational route for walkers and cyclists, and suitable for wheelchair users, maintained by the Snowdonia National Park Authority, which has provided information boards and picnic tables to enhance the user experience. The wide level surfaced trail offers close views of the tidal estuary, its saltmarsh and the birdlife it supports. After crossing the railway viaduct to reach Morfa Mawddach Halt on the southern side of the estuary, the wide surfaced Trail heads eastwards along the trackbed of the former Ruabon-Barmouth railway. After first passing through Arthog Bog the Trail follows closely the attractive open edge of the estuary. It passes the only two surviving native woodlands on this side of the estuary: Coed-y-Garth, which offers a 2 mile waymarked figure of eight trail which you may be tempted to incorporate in the walk, and Coed Abergwynant, owned and managed by Snowdonia National Park Authority. Eventually it reaches Penmaenpool with its historic toll bridge and the George III Hotel, where refreshments outside overlooking the river is highly recommended. The Trail continues through Penmaenpool Reeds, a Site of Special Scientific Interest, to Pont-y-Wernddu, where the trackbed ends, then follows a specially created surfaced route beside the Afon Wnion into Dolgellau.

1 Follow instructions in paragraph one of section 1 'Barmouth to Snowdonia National Park Arthog car park' on pages 12-16 then continue along the Mawddach Trail to a minor road by the Snowdonia National Park Arthog car park on the site of the former Arthog Station. (2¾ miles)

2 Please refer to the map on the following page for the next section of the Trail which now crosses an iron bridge over the tidal inlet then goes along the side of the estuary, whose saltmarsh is an important wildlife site for waders. After passing concrete 'tank traps' – *anti-invasion defences built during the Second World War* – the Trail continues along the attractive wooded edge of the estuary to an information board at the former Garth Siding, where once stood two cottages for railwaymen. *The demand for housing slate led to several quarries being opened in the hills adjoining the estuary. Ty'n y Coed quarry in nearby Arthog operated between 1860 and the early 1880s, when high costs forced its closure. Finished slate travelled from the cutting shed in trucks down an incline and along a tramway, to be taken away by sailing boat from a nearby jetty. Later it was taken from here by train.* The Trail continues past the remains of the old jetty and tramway, then crosses a bridge over the river. Later the estuary narrows – *where the clash between an incoming tide and the river is more evident. Debris adjoining the Trail indicates just how close the sea comes at certain high tides.* The Trail passes an information board on

Mawddach Trail

Coed-y-garth at the entrance to this regenerating oak woodland containing a waymarked figure of eight trail with panoramic views. The Trail continues briefly above the channel of the river as the estuary widens again. Later you reach another information board on Abergwynant where the Trail crosses a large bridge over the Afon Gwynant. *Here there is a good view across the estuary to Bontddu and Diffwys beyond.*

Please refer to the map on page 21 for the next section of the Trail which continues along the edge of the estuary past Abergwynant wood before bending away and heading directly east along a straight section of the former railway to reach the George III Hotel at Penmaenpool. For information see pages 21-22. (4½ miles)

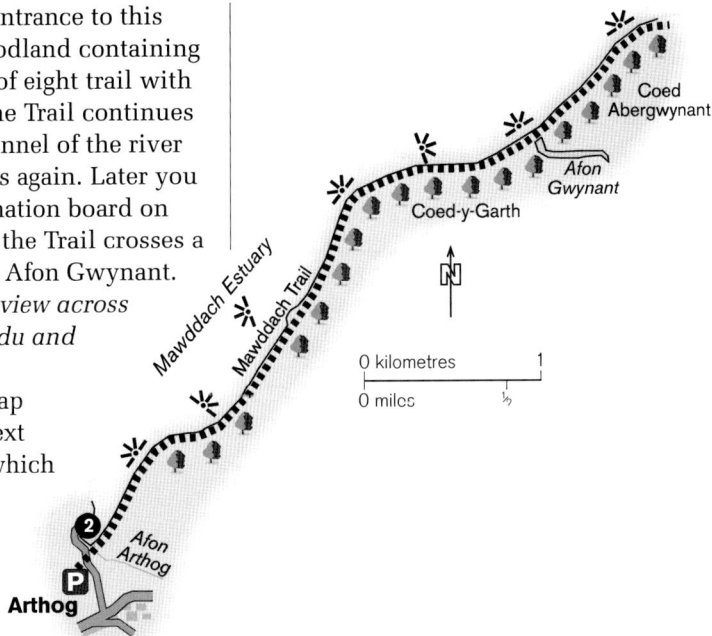

3 After refreshments at the George III continue on the Mawddach Trail to Dolgellau following instructions in paragraph 3 of Route A in section 3 on page 22.

Dolgellau

Dolgellau is a small historic market town standing at the foot of Cadair Idris mountain just beyond the eastern end of the long Mawddach valley. The origin of the town's name is uncertain, and it has had different spellings over the years. Coins found near the town indicate that the area was known to the Romans who may have been working nearby gold deposits. Dolgellau began as a small settlement in the 12thC at the junction of the Wnion and Aran rivers. Records indicate there was a church here in 1254 on the site of the present St Mary's church.

Owain Glyndŵr, who led a valiant revolt against English rule set up a senate in the town shortly before proclaiming the first Welsh Parliament in Machynlleth in 1404. After several years of fighting the revolt was eventually suppressed by superior forces, but Owain holds a special place in Welsh history. T H Roberts, a long established ironmongers and now a popular café, is said to stand on the site where Owain held his meetings.

The main entrance to the town is via the seven-arched stone bridge over the Wnion, known as 'Y Bont Fawr' (The Big Bridge) which was built in 1638. The bridge and its link to several ancient roads, enhanced the town's development. Dolgellau became an important stopping place on the packhorse and coach route from London to Harlech,

The town was also an important station on drovers routes, with cattle being shod here before starting their long journeys to southern England. The bridge was partly destroyed by a flood in 1903 and later was modified to accommodate the railway which arrived in 1864 and ran on the line of the present by-pass. The station was just upstream of the bridge.

The town's development is largely due to its prominent role in the area's manufacture of a coarse woollen cloth or flannel, called 'webs' or 'Welsh plains' in the 18th and 19th centuries. Mills and factories were built alongside the Afon Aran, which provided the power. Here, hand-woven cloth was beaten, washed, dried and bleached. The town became renowned for its cloth making. By the early 1840s about 1,400 people from Dolgellau and its vicinity were employed in the industry, making annually about 30,000 'webs', averaging 110 yards each. Until the end of the 18thC, in addition to land-carriage, cloth was transported along the river Wnion, then the Mawddach in small vessels to Barmouth, where it was transferred onto sea-going ships. One of the main markets was North America, where the coarse thick white cloth, shipped from Liverpool to Charleston and South Carolina, was used by slave owners and for making soldiers uniforms. After 1825 exports gradually declined but local trade continued. Tanning and printing were also important in the town's economy and during the 19thC it benefited from the gold rush in nearby hills and valleys. Until improvement in roads, then the arrival of the railway, the town was mainly supplied with goods and groceries shipped to Barmouth then brought in boats up to 20 tons

Eldon Square, Dolgellau

along the Mawddach as far as nearby Llanelltyd.

In the 17thC the town and local area played an important role in the development of the Quaker religion in Wales, but many Quakers emigrated to America to escape persecution. One of the earliest Grammar Schools in Wales was founded here in 1665.

As the town grew in importance it became the principal town of the old county of Merionethshire, now part of Gwynedd. Early in the 19thC the town centre was improved, creating Eldon Square, which became the social and commercial centre of the town. It was its meeting place and where markets, fairs and various community events were held. By the end of the 19thC the town boasted ten chapels as well as St Mary's church.

Dolgellau is a small town of irregular narrow streets of houses and tall buildings, some with huge chimneys, all built of the same local large stones. The close mixture of simple terraced cottages, wealthy town houses, fine public buildings and industrial buildings is so different to the planned layout of other towns that it it unique in Wales. Visitors in the 17th and 18thC apparently found these unappealing but by the early 19thC the town was beginning to attract tourists by offering interesting excursions to the surrounding area. Nearby Cadair Idris (Seat of Idris) was a main attraction, with climbing to its summit a popular activity. Today the town is fascinating to explore. A 'Town Trail' leaflet available from the Tourist Information Centre in Eldon Square will guide you to some of Dolgellau's most interesting historic buildings.

DOLGELLAU TO BARMOUTH
14¾ or 13¾ miles

The undulating return route to Barmouth along the northern side of the Mawddach estuary takes you through another stunning varied and historic landscape, full of interest with breathtaking views. It includes an alternative high level route which by-passes Bontddu, and a choice of routes before a final descent to Barmouth.

4 Dolgellau to Taicynhaeaf
4½ miles

The trail now heads north from Dolgellau to visit the ruins of Cymer Abbey (open daily and free admission) before crossing the Afon Mawddach into Llanelltyd, then rising up the part wooded hillside to the large hidden upland reservoir of Llyn Tan-y-Graig. From here it follows good paths up through a forest onto the open hillside to enjoy the New Precipice Walk – a former mine tramway contouring across the steep slopes beneath Foel Ispri, offering breathtaking views. Afterwards the trail descends through mixed woodland to the hamlet of Taicynhaeaf, lying at the foot of Cwm Mynach.

▌From Eldon Square follow the one-way road north through the town to cross the bridge over the river. At the junction turn left along the pavement to a Pelican crossing to join the pavement opposite. Go up nearby Ffordd Pen y Cefn past the school and houses, then the entrance to Plas Pen y Coed. *Just beyond there is a good view looking back across Dolgellau to Cadair Idris.* The road levels out and continues past further houses. At a junction turn left along the narrow road signposted to the golf club, soon descending past mixed woodland. At the entrance to the golf club on the left keep ahead to cross a stream then follow the signposted path along the left of two narrow tracks to a kissing gate/gate. Continue along the enclosed path, soon descending past a large stone ruin, to a road junction. Go along the no through road ahead – *once the main road* – then turn right, signposted to Cymer Abbey, along the driveway into Vanner caravan park. Shortly take the left fork to reach the farmhouse and the abbey ruins, now under the management of Cadw .

The Cistercian abbey was founded in 1198 under the patronage of Maredudd ap Cynan, grandson of Owain Gwynedd, Prince of Gwynedd and first occupied by monks from Abbey Cwmhir in Powys. The abbey stands on land adjacent to the old channel of the Afon Mawddach at a strategic crossing point of the river. To help sustain the colony the monks engaged in hill sheep farming and horse-breeding. Fishing supplemented their diet and upstream on the Mawddach are the

remains of several fish traps.
During the late 13thC it
was occupied by both
Welsh and English
troops and
suffered badly.
The abbey was
not a wealthy
one, earning just
£51 per annum
when in 1536 Henry
VIII included it in the list of
monasteries to be dissolved. This
is reflected in the simple design of
the abbey church, whose substantial
ruins are all that remain today, along
with part of the cloister. After the
Dissolution the abbey was abandoned
and periodically used as a source of
new building material. Some of the
abbey's decorated stone can be found
in the nearby farm buildings. The
farmhouse is said to have incorporated
part of the abbot's house. In the 19thC
a silver chalice and patten were
discovered nearby. They are believed
to have been hidden by the monks
at the time of the Dissolution. Now
part of a working farm, the tranquility
of the abbey's location can still be
appreciated.

Afterwards return through the caravan
park to the road. Turn right past the
Snowdonia National Park Authority
Llanelltyd car park, then cross the old
stone bridge over the Afon Mawddach.
For centuries this was the first bridged
crossing point of the river just above
where it is joined by the Afon Wnion
and broadens out into the estuary.
The present five arched stone bridge
on the site of earlier bridges dates to

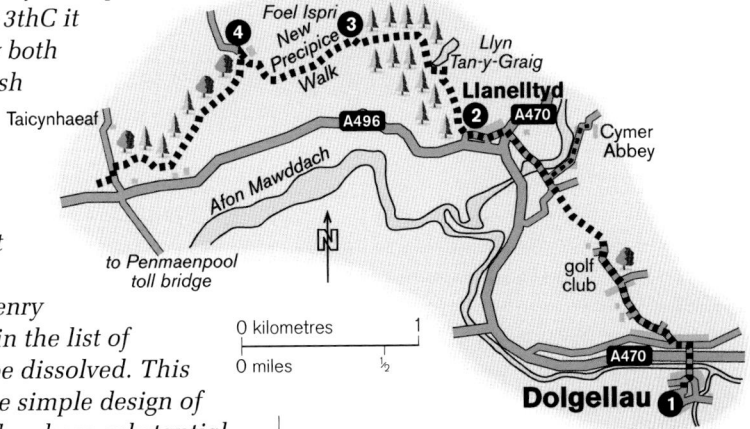

the second quarter of the 18thC and
carried the new Turnpike road between
Dolgellau and Barmouth which opened
in 1798, then the A470 trunk road
until a new concrete bridge was built
nearby in the 1980s. Continue along
the old road to a gate and on to reach
the A470. Cross the road with care to
the pavement opposite into Llanelltyd.
Now follow a road through the village
past houses and a chapel, then over
the river. In the 18th and early 19thC
small ship building yards were sited on
this side of the Mawddach estuary at
Llanelltyd and nearby Maes-y-garnedd.
The river was navigable for boats up to
20 tons from Barmouth as far as Maes-
y-garnedd, so it became an important
offloading point for supplies destined
for Dolgellau.

2 When the road finally bends
left to the nearby A496 go up
a signposted enclosed path on the
right. After a kissing gate the stony
path rises steadily beneath a forest.
At the end of the forest the path
continues up alongside the wall

31

now beneath deciduous trees. When it splits, take the path's stony left fork up the wooded slope – *soon with a view across to a ridge which carries the original Precipice Walk* – to a ladder-stile/gate into a more open area. Follow the path ahead to the nearby bend of a narrow green track. Bend right up the track, soon becoming a path, to a stile by Llyn Tan-y-Graig. *The large reservoir was built in the 19thC to provide water to power machines used in local mining operations.* Follow the path past the end of the lake into the forest, soon bending right and rising through the conifers then levelling out. After crossing a stream the path briefly rises again, then bends to a waymarked crossroad of paths. Take the path angling up through trees ahead – *soon with a view down to the river Mawddach.* The path continues up across the steep forested slope to a stream and a ladder-stile into open country.

3 Turn left alongside the wall to pass a ruined stone house at the forest corner. The path crosses a footbridge over a stream beneath small waterfalls, then goes up near the wall past another ruin. Continue with the path beside the wall to an old incline at a good viewpoint looking across Dolgellau to the Cadair Idris ridge beyond. The wide path now rises away from the wall to a gate at the start of the New Precipice Walk – *offering stunning views along the Mawddach estuary to the sea and across to the Cadair Idris range. Prominent in the valley below is the toll bridge at Penmaenpool.* The

delightful wide green path, a former tramway, contours across the steep hillside beneath Foel Ispri. *This small hill was extensively mined for minerals during the 19thC until the 1930s and the tramway was used to transport zinc, lead ore and a small amount of gold from the mine above. This superb section of exposed upland path is not to be rushed and I recommend that you take advantage of several seats for a break to take in the breathtaking views.* The path becomes edged by old railway lines to protect wheelchair users, who have access from a small car park at the other end. It then bends away from the Mawddach estuary – *with a view towards Diffwys and the Llawlech ridge* – and passes through small gates. Continue along a stony path to pass beneath Foel Ispri Uchaf cottage to another gate and on to nearby outbuildings. *Note the small waterwheel.*

4 At a small parking area just beyond the outbuildings do a sharp U-turn left down a wide waymarked path to a waymarked gate – *with a good view of Cadair Idris* – then down the wooded hillside to a stile/gate. The now narrow path continues down through woodland to a small metal gate, then down through trees, past a path descending left and another just beyond leading right from a wall corner. Continue ahead down the path through conifers, soon being joined by a wall on the right. Just before its corner the path bends left down through the conifers, crosses a stream, and continues down to a green track in a clearing. Follow it right for

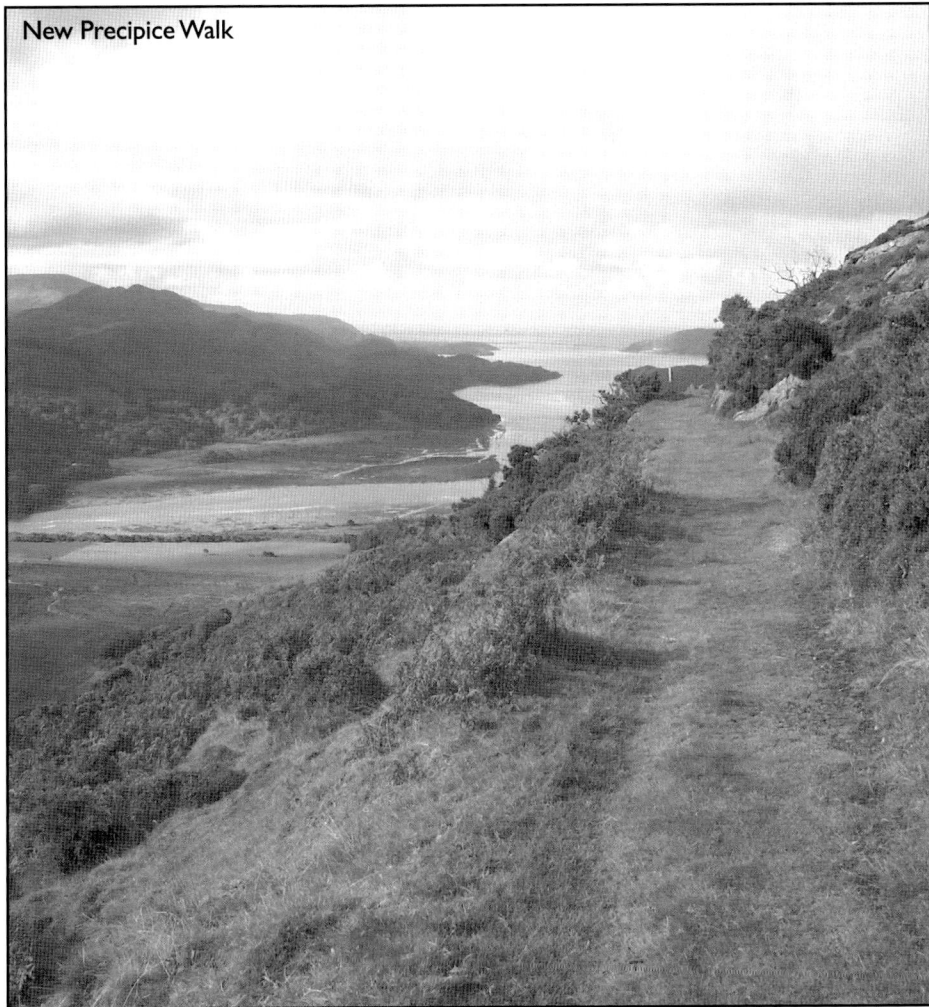

New Precipice Walk

a few yards then take the waymarked path on the left down through mixed woodland to a cross-path, with a gate opposite. Follow it right up alongside the wall then fence through mixed woodland, shortly levelling out to pass through a gap in a wall. Just beyond, the path angles right up through conifers, passes through a wall gap, then descends and continues to an old kissing gate in a wall. Follow the path ahead by a fence on the left, past a path on the right, down through deciduous trees. At the fence corner take the narrower left fork past the stile and down to a minor road in the hamlet of Taicynhaeaf at the bottom of Cwm Mynach – *the valley of the monks due to its association with land owned and used for sheep rearing by monks of Cymer Abbey.* Turn left down the road.

5 Taicynhaeaf to Bontddu
2¾ miles

From Taicynhaeaf the trail follows the Afon Cwm-mynach up the beautiful narrow wooded valley along the eastern edge of RSPB Coed Garth Gell Nature Reserve on a former tramway to an old mill used in gold mining. The main trail then follows a good path south through the delightful predominantly oak woodland Reserve past good viewpoints, before descending to the A496 and continuing along the edge of the Mawddach estuary to Bontddu. From the Reserve's northern edge there is an alternative upland route direct to Pont Hirgwm above Bontddu which will reduce the overall distance by 1⅓ mile. Separate detailed instructions are provided later.

1 Take a signposted enclosed path on the right down past a house to a bridge over the Afon Cwm-mynach into woodland. Go past a gate and follow the path up alongside a low wall/fence to a narrow stony track by a gateway. Turn right and follow the track up above the river tumbling down the narrow beautiful wooded gorge. *The track is a former tramway from the gold mine further up the valley, which was worked between 1865-1902. It follows the edge of the Coed Garth Gell Nature Reserve, which consists of predominantly sessile oak woodland, bog myrtle and upland heath, providing a rich habitat for a wide range of plants and animals.* The track rises steadily through the delightful wooded valley, gradually

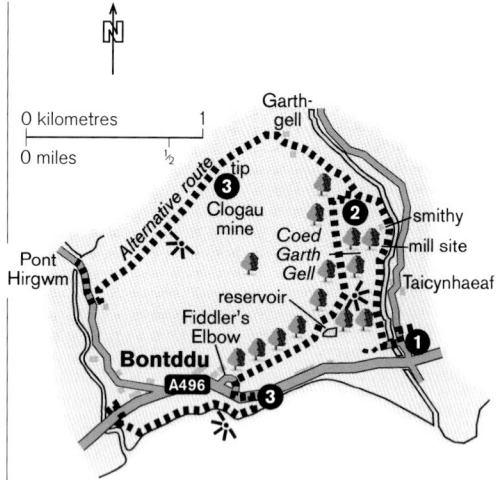

becoming more a path in nature. You pass a railed path down to the former mill site where the ore was crushed. *By the river are the remains of six circular buddles, which were filled with mercury to separate the metal from crushed rock. In the valley gold prospectors found a hoard of 13thC religious silverware, now in National Museum in Cardiff.* The path continues up the wooded valley to the former smithy, then through the attractive woodland of oak, birch and rowan, soon above the river once more. It passes an old mine entrance on the left, then moves away from the river again to reach a ladder-stile/gate by an information board at the perimeter of the Coed Garth Gell Nature Reserve.

2 Do not cross the ladder-stile but turn left on the signed green path up nearby steps and follow the path near the wall, soon bending left away from it up to a small gate in another wall. After a few yards the path bends right through trees, soon rising, to

Mawddach Estuary

reach a waymark post at a public footpath. Turn left across the stream and continue through the woodland reserve, past a bench seat in a more open area, after which the path rises through trees and continues to a small metal gate in a wall. The path now descends through a gap in a wall and passes a good viewpoint across the estuary to Penmaenpool. After further estuary views the path descends more steeply through woodland. When the path splits at a waymark post, where the blue trail leads left to nearby Ceonfa reservoir, continue down the right fork to join a wall to leave the Reserve by a small gate. The path continues beside the wall down through woodland. Go past an old iron gate in it and continue beside the wall to go through another small gate onto the adjoining access lane. Follow it down to Fiddler's Elbow car park and picnic area. Cross the A490 to a lay-by opposite and turn left through it, then go along a short section of road verge by the barrier.

3 At its end turn right on a signposted path down the driveway to Rhuddallt. After a gate just before the house turn left down to a waymarked gate. Go past a building, then at a cross-path turn right to another gate, then follow the waymarked path above the estuary and on to a kissing gate/gate – *enjoying great views along the estuary to the sea.* Continue along a track past the reedy edge of the estuary. At a track junction keep ahead, past a seat made out of a tree trunk then another track on the right – *with a good view across the estuary to the Cadair Idris ridge and east to Penmaenpool toll bridge and other mountains.* After the track bends right and just before a gate, go down a waymarked path to cross a small footbridge over a tidal watercourse and through a gate. Continue with the waymarked path near a fence across tussocky terrain, then past woodland to a kissing gate. Go along a stony track beside the river Hirgwm. When it bends towards gates follow a path ahead through trees, briefly alongside the river, then bending right to join a driveway which you follow up to the main road in Bontddu. Cross to the pavement opposite and turn left, then go along a narrow road beneath houses adjoining the main road and past a nearby bus shelter.

Alternative route from Taicynhaeaf to Pont Hirgwm avoiding Bontddu

2½ miles

After following the main trail above the Afon Cwm-mynach up the beautiful narrow wooded valley this route continues north west, partly on a courtesy path (closed 5th February each year) created by Snowdonia National Park Authority with the local landowner, to remote Garth Gell, where it connects with public rights of way. It then rises across upland pasture to an old gold mining area, from where it descends a former tramway into Cwm Hirgwm.

1 Follow instructions in paragraph one of section 5.

2 At the northern perimeter of Coed Garth Gell Reserve cross the ladder-stile and follow a green path ahead across the reedy/bracken covered ground, soon rising steadily – *with a good open view up Cwm Mynach* – to a kissing gate to join a courtesy path beyond. It follows an old gated track beside the boundary then rises to a gate at Garth Gell. Go through the gate and angle left to pass between the end of the house and an outbuilding, then follow the waymarked path up a green track. When it bends left follow the waymarked path to a wall gap ahead, then go up the reedy/tussocky terrain a little way from woodland on your right to rejoin the track just before a gate and kissing gate in a wall into Open Access land. Follow the green track up open pasture to level out at a waymark post on the skyline. Here angle left on the waymarked bridleway, soon alongside a wall on the left – *with a good view ahead of the mouth of the estuary.* The wall continues to where it joins another, which you follow right and round to a ladder-stile in it, but you need to move away from the wall to circumvent a small wet reedy area adjoining it. *You now have a good view down into Cwm Hirgwm and across to the Llawlech ridge.*

3 Cross the ladder-stile. *Nearby is a tip and drainage adit for one of two new mines worked in the late 1850s/early 1860s. On top of the hill is the Old Clogau copper and gold mine. By 1865, a system of tramways and inclines were being built around the mountain to transport ore down to Figra Mill.* Turn right and follow a delightful old level tramway through two gates and on to a waymark post, where the tramway splits. Go down the long right fork – *enjoying views to the estuary* – to a kissing gate. Continue with the old tramway down the hillside, passing through a gate. When it levels out, just before a gate and nearby cottage, bend sharp right down an enclosed path onto a road. Follow it right to Pont Hirgwm, where you join the main route at point 2 of section.

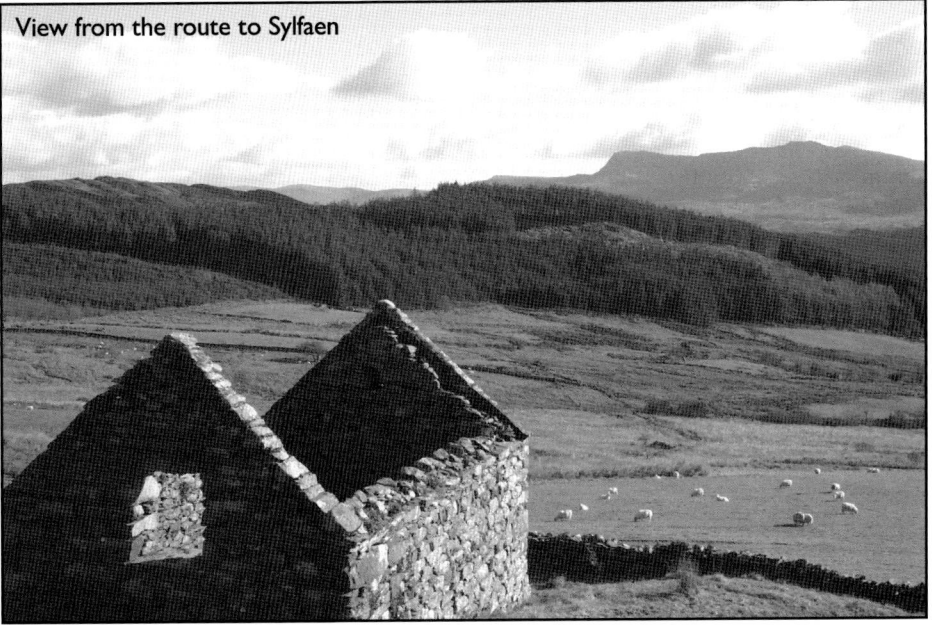

View from the route to Sylfaen

6 Bontddu to Sylfaen

4 miles

This delightful section of the trail follows in the footsteps of travellers, drovers, gold prospectors and church worshippers, who used a network of ancient upland highways across the hills, upland valleys and mountains above Bontddu, some of which once echoed to the sound of mining. This section first takes you up through the impressive wooded Hirgwm gorge, past the site of a crushing mill used in gold production then the entrance to the famous Clogau gold mine. From Pont Hirgwm the trail rises steadily by minor road, part of the old London-Dolgellau-Harlech highway, along the edge of the Hirgwm valley into high upland pasture. It then follows one of the branches of the former ancient road, initially a bridleway then a track across a wide upland valley at just over 800 feet beneath bare foothills. As the old highway starts to rise to a high pass, the trail continues along a wide scenic track, offering panoramic views of the Cadair Idris mountain range, to Sylfaen, a large upland farm. For much of the way the trail follows part of the ancient route taken by inhabitants of Bontddu on their arduous 5 mile walk via Bwlch y Llan to the 13th C parish church in Llanaber.

Bontddu owes its development alongside the former Turnpike road to the 19thC gold mining boom which attracted companies to explore the area above the village for this precious metal. The steep-sided Hirgwm valley and surrounding hills became one of the most important gold-mining areas in Britain. Small-scale mining, primarily for copper and lead, probably occurred here since

37

before the Romans. Between 1825-45, Figra and Old Clogau mines, on opposite sides of the valley, were worked for copper. But a chance discovery of gold, worth thousand of pounds, on a spoil tip in 1854 led to the first of several gold rushes. The working of the gold

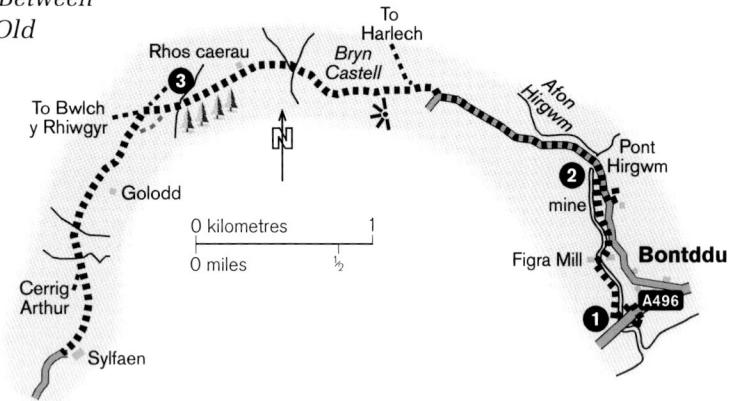

bearing quartz veins, primarily the St David's Lode, during the rest of the century, in what became known as the Clogau Mine, was undertaken by a series of companies, some shortlived. A gold rush in 1862 saw the existing company awarded a medal at the Great Exhibition. From 1898 to the early 1900s, mining was larger in scale, involving up to 63 men working above ground and 190 below, and producing a peak yield of 18,417 oz of gold in 1904. Mining has continued intermittently since then, producing the famous Clogau gold used to make wedding rings for the Royal Family. Most gold extraction involved adit mining – inclined tunnels driven by hand – until the 1870s when compressed-air drills were introduced. They provided access to the ore, drainage and ventilation.

Until the building of Turnpike roads in the late 18th and early 19thC, enabling good access along the Mawddach estuary and the coast, travelling and moving goods by pack horse between Harlech and Dolgellau,

linking with other roads to London, was difficult and challenging. It required following ancient highways, possibly prehistoric in origin, across the mountains. Drovers also used these routes to move cattle from the coast near Harlech on their way to markets in England. Rising from Bontddu an important ancient road, which was later used by horse-drawn coaches, divides into two branches. One went to Harlech via Bwlch y Rhiwgyr and Tal-y-bont. The other took a shorter more direct route, but over a higher pass, to reach Harlech via Pont Scethin and Llanbedr, and may have been a summer route. It is also speculated that this well constructed route is a Roman road. During the 18thC, when local gentry were becoming increasingly anglicised, the old road was an important link via Dolgellau to London Society. Improvements to the old road were made in 1765 at the request of William Vaughan of Cors y Gedol, near Tal-y-bont .

1 After crossing the old bridge over the river Hirgwm go up the no through road past toilets and houses, then continue up a stony track above the impressive deep narrow wooded river gorge to level out at the remains of Figra mill.

The mill, powered by a waterwheel, was built as a crushing mill to serve the copper mines, then adapted for gold production in 1862. A zig-zag track and incline connected the mill with Figra mine above. There were constant changes in machinery to improve the extraction of gold from pulverised quartz and reduce the gold being lost in the process. Mechanical crushing was done by 'stamps', heavy columns of wood and iron, requiring massive foundations and reinforcement of the river bank. At the end of the 19th C a new mill powered by a turbine was built, with a gas engine as standby. Just downstream was a smaller mill in use until the 1930s, whose Britten pans used mercury to extract the fine gold particles. In the 1890s high grade ore was brought here in locked boxes by Robin the donkey!

Cross nearby Figra Bridge over the river. Bear left up the stony path past a track leading to nearby houses, then follow the stony track ahead up the eastern side of the wooded valley, shortly levelling out to pass the secured entrance to Clogau mine – *first worked in 1862, and connected by Llechfraith adit to the main workings on Clogau mountain in 1903.* After a kissing gate/gate continue up a path through a more open area, briefly above the river, to a kissing gate onto a minor road. Turn left to cross nearby Pont Hirgwm, near the entrance to Dwynant/ Ty-Glan-Afon.

2 Continue up the attractive narrow road – *the ancient highway to Harlech and also part of the church route to Llanaber* – past an access road on the right, then briefly close by the river and past Tynlonuchaf. After a cattle-grid the road passes the entrances to Caegoronwy and Cae Hir, then continues to rise into more open country – *with a good view of the Diffwys ridge and, looking back, of Cadair Idris* – shortly levelling out. When it bends left and becomes a stony track go through a bridle gate on the right and follow the signposted bridleway up near a wall, soon bending away and rising up a gorse-covered slope, guided by small white-topped posts. You reach a large inscribed milestone, marking the two branches of the old road to Harlech. *The right fork climbs up to a high mountain pass then descends to cross Pont Scethin, a remote ancient bridge which the trail crosses on another day.* Go up the left fork, inscribed Tal-y-bont, to a ladder-stile/gate. The old road, now little more than a path, continues beside a wall – *with a view along the Mawddach estuary to Fairbourne and the sea* – down to a gate, The path then descends, rejoining the wall and passing above a substantial ruined stone barn – *with the Llawlech ridge ahead. On nearby Bryn Castell is an ancient hillfort, and a medieval settlement.* Shortly the path joins another wall and heads towards the bare ridge to a ladder-

The point where the old Harlech road splits

stile/gate. The path descends, and continues to cross the Afon Dwynant, then accompanies the fence-topped wall to an iron gate. It then passes the ruin of Rhos caerau on the right – *a former staging post that once provided refreshments for passing travellers* – and joins a green track which passes a plantation, becoming increasingly closer to the southern slopes of the ridge.

3 After going through a gate at the plantation corner and crossing a stream just beyond the stonier track continues across open ground, past a green track on the left and over another stream. At a small white topped post, where the track bends half-left towards a gate, keep straight ahead alongside a stream to cross a stone stile in the wall onto a green cross track just beyond. *The old road to Harlech rises up the hillside ahead to Bwlch y Rhiwgyr before continuing to Tal-y-bont. In the 18th and early 19thC peat cut upon the*

mountain top was brought down the old road in trucks on sleds. Turn left along the green track to rejoin the wide part stony track – *with a good view of the Cadair Idris range.* The track heads south west across the expansive upland valley – *still on the old route to Llanaber church* – through two gates in quick succession, then continues past a ruin and the remains of Golodd below – *said to be where drovers left their cattle. Higher up the slope to your right, beyond a wall, is the next section of the trail from Barmouth to Bwlch y Rhiwgyr.* The track passes through two further gates – *after which the old church route heads up to Cerrig Arthur stone circle before continuing via Bwlch-y-Llan to Llanaber.* Continue along the stony track past a small quarry – *soon with a good view of the estuary* – to another gate and down past a side track and large barn to join a minor road at the entrance to Sylfaen farm.

7 Sylfaen to Barmouth
3½ or 2½ miles

The next section offers two equally interesting routes to Dinas Oleu with stunning views, before a final breathtaking descent into Barmouth.

Route A (2½ miles) ontinues along the scenic upland road then follows paths up to a hillside transmitter mast (918 ft/280 metres) and across upland pasture, before descending in stages to Dinas Oleu. Although higher and more exposed this route features delightful paths and panoramic mountain and estuary views throughout.

Route B (3½ miles) has more historical interest and includes one of the area's classic viewpoints overlooking the Mawddach estuary. The route descends in stages through woodland to the hidden hamlet of Cutia just above the northern edge of the estuary, before following a delightful former narrow walled 17thC highway across wooded slopes to visit the classic Panorama Walk viewpoint. It then continues to Dinas Oleu. This lower and more sheltered approach is a better option in bad weather and poor visibility.

Route A

Go down the road and follow it past houses – *enjoying good views of the Mawddach estuary and the long Cadair Idris ridge. Beneath the ridge just to the west is the first stage of the Ardudwy Way descending from Bwlch y Llan.* After almost ½ mile, as the road

bends left take the signposted path ahead up to a ladder-stile/gate. The path now rises up the hillside towards the transmitter mast, becoming increasingly enclosed by walls. After a small gate – *with a good view looking back to Sylfaen and Diffwys* – the path continues up alongside a wall, then just before a gate in the corner turn right up alongside another wall past the transmitter mast and buildings to a ladder-stile and small gate into Open Access land. *The path rising ahead leads up to the top of Bwlch y Llan, which you will be passing through on the next stage of the trail.* Turn left and follow a path alongside the wall to a ladder-stile/old iron gate. Turn left again and follow the waymarked path – *with Cadair Idris ahead* – soon moving away from the wall and bending right to a wall gap. Continue along the level path – *enjoying panoramic estuary and mountain views* – soon near a wall, then passing through a wall gap. The delightful path then makes a long steady descent to a gate onto a minor road. *On the descent you will enjoy superb views across the railway viaduct at the mouth of the estuary to Fairbourne and the coast beyond, then inland along the estuary itself. Down to your left overlooking the estuary is the Panorama Walk.*

2 Turn right along the narrow scenic road to a ladder-stile/gate, then continue up the road. When it bends right, turn left on the signposted path. The path descends beneath 'The Slabs' – *a popular location for rock climbing* – to a small iron gate, then continues down past a fenced off area to another similar gate. The path continues to descend, bending left briefly near a wall then down to an old iron gate in it. Follow the path to a waymarked path junction near a seat at a good viewpoint overlooking the railway viaduct and the mouth of the estuary.

Route B

Go down the road then just after the road bends right and starts to level out go through a gate on the left at a good viewpoint across the estuary to Cadair Idris. Go down the stony track to a large stone barn. Go through the right of two facing gates below the barn and on through a gate ahead at its far end into a field. Now follow the wall on your right down past an old gate, to go through a waymarked facing gate just beyond. Follow a path down beside the wall then through trees, soon bending right then left. The path continues down through woodland, past a section of wall, and on to reach a waymark post at a cross-path leading to a nearby low stone stile on the left. Here turn right and follow the path through woodland to a ladder-stile/ gate and on to another ladder-stile beyond a fast-flowing stream. The path now descends through the wood to a ladder-stile/ gate. Continue with the wide path through the more open woodland of Coed y Tyn Llidiart, then at a crossroad of paths turn left down alongside a wall past a pylon and follow the path to a small gate. Pass between a house and the former Cutia chapel up to your right, now privately owned. *The old chapel has an interesting history. It was built in 1806,* *when the Congregationalists began teaching their doctrine locally. One of its prime promoters was a Mr Evans, originally from Llangollen, who opened a school in Barmouth to teach basic education and the gospel. On Sundays, he preached in Barmouth, Cutia, and Dyffryn, a commitment which affected his health. In 1826, members of the three communities asked that he serve as their pastor. Their written request included the enticement of 'regarding your sustenance, we of Cutiau promise to collect 8 pounds a year'. At the time the chapel contained 20 members. He was only 24 years old, when he was ordained here on 23rd May 1827. Later a new chapel was built in Barmouth, and he travelled throughout Wales, raising £300 towards its cost of £600. In 1844, the Rev. James Jones took over, cleared the rest of the debt, and offered a bilingual service to English nonconformist visitors.*

Go along its narrow walled access lane, then descend a narrow road through the hamlet of Cutia. When the road bends down sharp left, with a telegraph pole and large white painted iron gate ahead, turn right and follow a delightful narrow walled track through Coed Glan-y-Mawddach. *It is a section of the 17th Dolgellau to Barmouth road, used by travellers and later the Royal Mail before the building of the turnpike road in 1798, now the A496.* At a signposted path junction go up the right fork alongside a wall. This delightful path rises steadily through the wood – *with an early glimpse through the trees of the nearby estuary. Shortly it passes above the large ruin of Bwlch-y-Goedleoedd, reputed to* be an old inn. The great 14thC Welsh poet, Dafydd ap Gwilym apparently stayed here. It is said that after his plan to meet 12 local young women at different times was discovered, he gladly retreated to his locked room at the inn!

2 Just before a wooden gate go through an iron gate on the left giving access to the Panorama Walk. *This short walk to a magnificent viewpoint over the estuary was created in the late 19thC as a tourist attraction. In the early 1880s, a penny was charged by Mr Davies of the Corsygedol Hotel for entry via a 'toll-wicket' here, causing people to grumble and write to the papers. A commentator at the time said that without his enterprise the 'View' would have been lost to the public altogether! In the early 20thC there was a cafe here.* Follow the path through the trees, soon rising, then go up its left fork past a seat to emerge onto the open hillside and reach another seat at a stunning viewpoint. *There are extensive views along the estuary east beyond Penmaenpool to the distant Aran mountains and to the west the railway viaduct at its mouth, and the coast extending from Fairbourne.* Follow the path towards the sea – *with new views down to the Fairbourne railway terminus opposite Barmouth harbour* – down steps, then down through trees to rejoin the outward path. After going through the large iron gate turn left through the nearby wooden gate and up the the wide walled path to emerge from the wood. Continue on the open path,

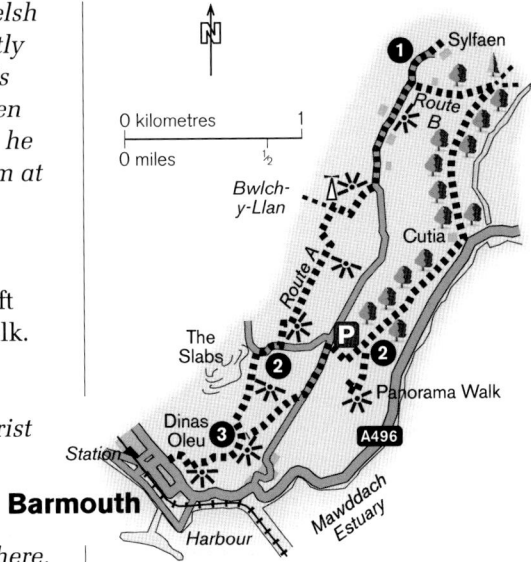

soon descending to pass a large stone barn then rising to an iron gate onto Panorama Road. Turn left down the road, past a stony access track rising to Bryn Derw on the right opposite a track leading down to Hafod-y-Bryn. Shortly take a signposted path angling up an access track on the right. At a gate just before the house, turn right up steps to a kissing gate and follow the path beside the fence. At its corner above a cottage, turn left down the wide walled path to a gate. Continue up past a house, and at another ahead turn right along a walled track to a gate between stone outbuildings. Continue up the stony track, soon levelling out, then becoming tarmaced and descending to the gated entrance to Caefadog. Here, turn right to go through a nearby small iron gate. Take the path rising across the slope ahead to join Route A at a waymarked path junction by a seat.

43

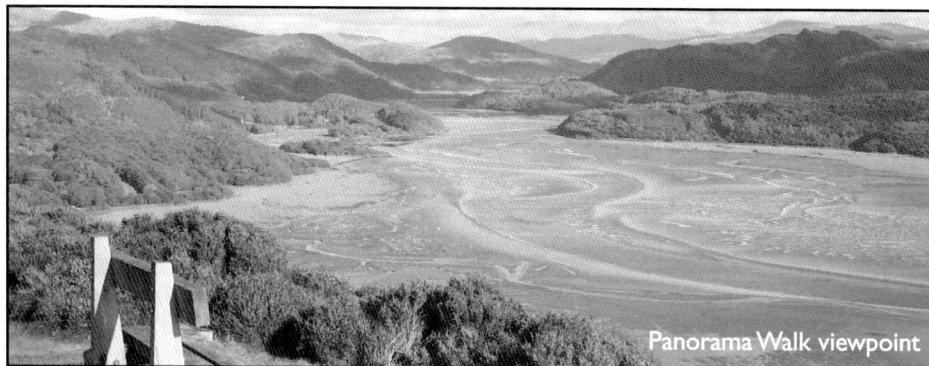

Panorama Walk viewpoint

The descent to Barmouth

The seat makes a good place for a stop to enjoy the breathtaking views and reflect on your journey around the Mawddach estuary before the final descent to Barmouth. In addition to the Cambrian Coast railway you can see the Fairbourne narrow gauge railway and its terminus opposite Barmouth harbour. Also visible on the far side of the estuary are the remains of the hillside slate quarry at Arthog and a row of large three storey terraced houses of Mawddach Crescent by the estuary edge, built as part of the ambitious plans by Solomon Andrews to develop the nearby area into a major seaside resort.

3 From the seat continue west along the path beside the perimeter wall of Dinas Oleu. The rugged hillside overlooking Barmouth was the first property given to the National Trust after its foundation in 1895. It was donated by Mrs Fanny Talbot and aptly fulfils the stated desire of creating 'open-air sitting rooms for city dwellers to have a place to breathe'. She also gave thirteen cottages to her close friend, writer, art critic and social reformer John Ruskin to further his experiments in social living. One of his first tenants was Auguste Guyard, known locally as 'The Frenchman' He worked tirelessly, instructing local people on horticultural matters and the virtues of a frugal industrious life, until his death in 1883. He is buried on the hillside. Mothers used to bring children suffering from whooping cough onto Dinas Goleu to benefit from the seaborne air. Continue past the gated entrance to the Frenchman's Grave and down to a small gate overlooking Barmouth with its expansive beach at low tide. Follow the path ahead meandering down the hillside – offering extensive views of Barmouth, its harbour and distant Llyn peninsula – soon joined by a path from the right, to reach an information board on Dinas Oleu overlooking the old town. Follow a wide stony path leading right down the hillside to join a narrow lane beneath houses. Follow it down, soon joined by another lane, then bending left to a junction. Turn right along Water Street to reach the main street in the centre of Barmouth.

BARMOUTH TO LLANBEDR
14½ miles

8 Barmouth to above Pont Fadog
5¾ miles

The trail now joins the waymarked Ardudwy Way as it begins its journey north across an fascinating upland area, important since prehistoric times, featuring two ancient mountain passes and highways, Bronze Age monuments and extensive views. It rises quickly from the town then continues by paths and delightful green tracks up to the top of Bwlch y Llan (1148 ft/350 metres) before gradually descending to Cerrig Arthur Stone Circle. It then climbs to Bwlch y Rhiwgyr (1509 ft /460 metres) from where it follows an ancient route across a treeless upland landscape containing cairns and stone circles.

I From the railway station/Tourist Information Centre go along the left-hand pavement of nearby Station Road towards the large St John's church passing an information board on the Ardudwy Way. At the junction with the main street cross to the road opposite and follow it round left then right up to where it is line with St. John's church. Here turn left up narrow Gellfechan Road. When it levels out – *with a good view overlooking Barmouth* – turn right on the signposted Ardudwy Way. Follow the wide green path, soon rising steadily,

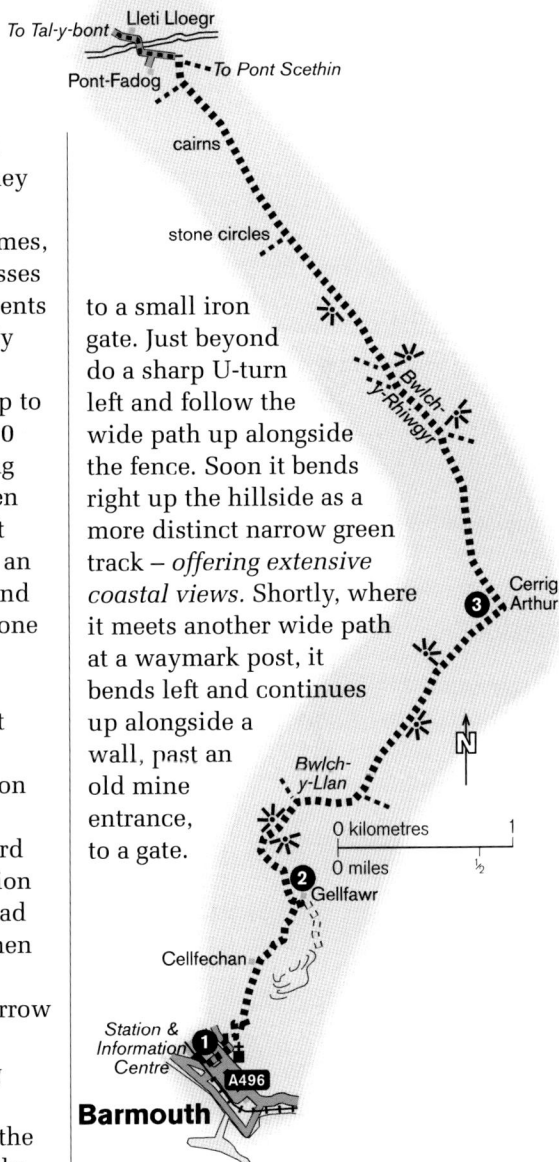

to a small iron gate. Just beyond do a sharp U-turn left and follow the wide path up alongside the fence. Soon it bends right up the hillside as a more distinct narrow green track – *offering extensive coastal views*. Shortly, where it meets another wide path at a waymark post, it bends left and continues up alongside a wall, past an old mine entrance, to a gate.

To Tal-y-bont
Lleti Lloegr
Pont-Fadog
To Pont Scethin
cairns
stone circles
Bwlch-y-Rhiwgyr
Cerrig Arthur **3**
N
Bwlch-y-Llan
0 kilometres   1
0 miles   ½
2 Gellfawr
Cellfechan
Station & Information Centre **1**
A496
Barmouth

The track you are following served the hillside manganese mines that were worked in the late 19th and early 20thC. Manganese was mainly used in the production of hardened steel. Continue up the delightful green track. *Nearby to your left is a small cairn with a Welsh flag on the small heather/tree covered outlying top of Craig-y-Gigfran (Ravens Rock). On the cairn is a plaque erected to the memory of soldiers from Birmingham killed in 1916.* Go past a large stone ruin at Cellfechan farm. *In the 1920s the farm was owned by the Urban District Council and provided refreshments to passing walkers.* At the waymarked path junction keep ahead up the path to go through a narrow gap in a wall by a post. At another waymarked path junction beyond angle right with the Ardudwy Way up alongside a wall to cross a stone stile. Turn left up the path near the wall, soon descending to pass through a wall gap and continuing down to a waymarked path junction near a gateway in the wall. Turn right a few yards then angle left through reeds to a stream and a small iron gate. Continue alongside the fence. At its corner turn right and follow a green track past a ruin to Gellfawr.

2 Turn left along a narrow green track to pass between outbuildings, then follow the delightful track – *associated with local manganese mining* – up the attractive upland area to a ladder-stile/gate. Continue with the track – *enjoying good views to Shell Island and the Llyn peninsula* – to another ladder-stile/gate. The Ardudwy Way now heads right on a steady climb up Bwlch y Llan (Pass to the Church). *For the next section to Cerrig Arthur you are following part of the ancient route used by inhabitants of Bontddu – a distance of over 5 miles – to worship in the 13thC parish church overlooking the coast at Llanaber.* At the top of the pass follow the path round and across a small ridge to a ladder-stile by a gate. Follow the path ahead – *enjoying a good view of the Mawddach estuary and Cadair Idris beyond* – soon descending to a ladder-stile, then to a gate by sheepfolds. Keep ahead, past a ruined stone barn and on to a gate in the wall corner to reach the remains of Carreg Arthur stone circle beyond.

Cerrig Arthur, set high on the open hillside, is the remains of a Bronze Age circle, possibly a ritual or burial monument. Interestingly, the stones stand near the original site planned for Llanaber church, and are known as 'Church Stones'. According to tradition, the church's foundations were repeatedly demolished at night by an unseen power. The subsequent hearing of a voice crying "Llanaber, Llanaber'" made the terrified men change the location for their parish church. The ancient church route now heads down to join the wide track followed in section 6 of the trail.

3 Now turn left and follow the Ardudwy Way up to a gate, then continue up a green track to join a wall on your left. Shortly, go through a gate in the wall. Turn right and follow a path just above the wall. Later angle slightly away to a stile in an old gateway. Go through wall gap ahead, then angle left up the tussocky slope to a gate. Follow the green track up to an iron gate at the top of Bwlch y Rhiwgyr (Pass of the Drovers). *Here you are joined by the old road from Bontddu, part of the London to Harlech highway you left earlier on the way to Sylfaen farm. This high mountain pass has been used since man first came to this area, as evidenced by the remains of a large Bronze Age cairn a short distance upslope to the right partly buried under a wall.* Go through the gate and follow the stony path down the narrow pass to a gate and on down to another. The Ardudwy Way then continues beside a boundary, later becoming a narrow green track. *Just beyond a path on the left in an adjoining field, are the remains of two Bronze Age stone circles. Further along the track, just to the west are the remains of another stone circle and cairns. Such a concentration of Bronze Age monuments used for ritual or community purposes accessed or seen from the ancient trackway from Bwlch y Rhiwgyr indicate the importance of this upland area in prehistoric times.* After two ladder-stiles the track descends across open ground to a track junction, almost two miles from Bwlch y Rhiwgyr. *The old road to Tal-y-bont continues through the gate ahead, whilst the Ardudwy Way heads east up along Cwm Ysgethin. The nearby Scots pines were a traditional means of guiding drovers during the 17th and 18th centuries to Lleti Loegr – an emergency shoeing station and overnight stopping place just beyond Pont Fadog.*

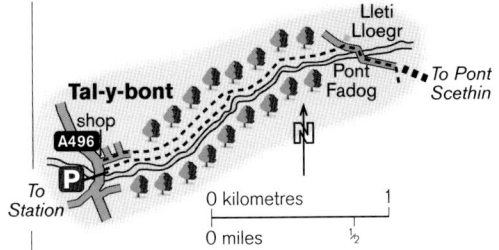

Link to Tal-y-bont
1½ miles

Go down the track ahead then follow the narrow road down to cross Pont Fadog over the Afon Ysgethin. *A stone inscription on the former packhorse bridge dates it 1762 and names H Ed(ward) as the mason employed by William Vaughan of nearby Cors y Gedol.* Continue up the lane then take a signposted bridleway opposite Lleti Lloegr. Follow the bridleway down through the trees to a small gate then above the river past side paths to a junction by a seat. Continue with the left fork down the attractive wooded valley to a ladder-stile/gate, then past two footbridges and a small stone building to reach the Ysgethin Inn. *The porch of this former late 19thC woollen mill was built with stone taken from an old drover's inn, Rhos-caerau, on the upland route to Bontddu.* Continue on a wide path beside the river to reach a small car park, toilets and bus stop in Tal-y-bont.

To rejoin the trail you can simply return the same way up the wooded Yscethin valley or for a variation follow the route now described. From the toilets and car park go up adjoining Llwyn Ynn. Just past the second road on the left take a signposted path up a narrow road on the right above the wooded valley. At the entrance to Daquin continue ahead along a path on the top edge of the wooded valley to a gate. The wide path continues to rise steadily above the wooded valley. At a path junction follow the wide path ahead to join the main valley route at a familiar seat.

Descent from Bwlch y Rhiwgyr

9 Above Pont Fadog to Ffynnon Enddwyn

5 miles

The next section continues with the Ardudwy Way on an undulating exposed upland route following ancient tracks and paths past sites of historic interest and featuring another highlight of the trail – the ancient stone bridge of Pont Scethin set in splendid isolation at 1036 feet beneath the foothills of the Rhinogs. The trail first follows an old drovers route up and across the wild expansive treeless upland valley of Cwm Ysgethin past hidden Llyn Erddyn set beneath the Llawlech ridge. It then joins the other branch of the former Harlech-London road to cross Pont Scethin. After following the old road for a further 1½ miles, passing beneath Moelfre, the trail continues across upland pasture to Ffynnon Enddwyn, an ancient healing well situated just below a minor road.

▌At the track junction turn right and follow the track up to a gate, then up to another into Open Access land. The track continues to rise steadily, passing through two further gates – *with extensive views looking back* – before heading along the expansive valley to another gate. *Just to the north on Craig y Dinas, an isolated small rocky knoll is an impressive Iron Age hillfort and the remains a settlement of round houses on lower ground outside. It is thought that the fort itself was a place of refuge or a communal*

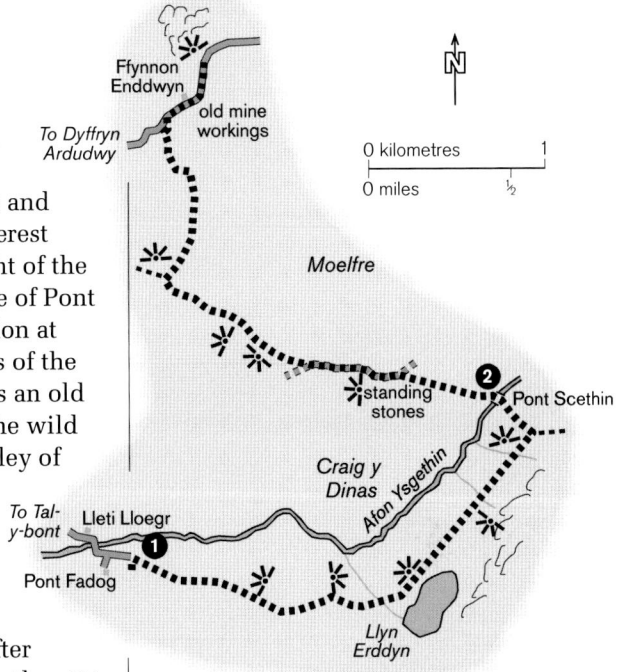

meeting place. Continue with the track to skirt the north western side of Llyn Erddyn still hidden by a small rise. *In the mid 19thC the trout caught here before sunrise were considered to be the best in the area. It is known as the 'priest lake' from its association with Druids, who reputedly used the large stones along its banks as seats for worshipping, and kept a store of fish at its outlet.* After another gate continue along the old track – *after a while looking back to see Llyn Erddyn* – to a gate. Keep ahead along the track's left fork, over a stream and on through the wide reedy valley – *with your first sight of Pont Scethin.* Eventually you reach a wide cross path. *This is the old London–Harlech road which*

Pont Scethin

you last saw at the large inscribed stone marking the two branches of the upland highway in section 6 of the trail from Bontddu. It is hard to imagine stage coaches passing through this inhospitable exposed upland landscape, especially as it involved a crossing of a high pass (1837 ft/560 metres) on the nearby Llawlech ridge. Follow the old road left down to Pont Scethin – *an important crossing point of the Afon Ysgethin on this ancient road, used for centuries by travellers and later drovers. It is a delightful place to stop to enjoy the solitude of this remote stone bridge and dippers in the river.*

2 Continue on the line of the old road rising steadily up the hillside. *When it levels out, look for two small prehistoric standing stones on your left.* The old road then joins a wide track beneath the southern slopes

of Moelfre. *The track services Llyn Bodlyn reservoir further up the valley.* Here turn left down the track. After ⅓ mile as it bends down to a gate in a wall take the waymarked Ardudwy Way angling right to a nearby iron gate. Follow a path above an old reedy track – *the old Harlech road* – across the base of Moelfre – *with good views across Cardigan Bay to the Llyn peninsula* – then continue with the wide path parallel with a wall. At its corner continue beside the old reedy track, shortly joining it to go through a gate in a wall – *with views to the large sand dunes on Shell Island and to distant Criccieth.* Continue down the green track. Shortly, at a gateway you leave the old road by turning right on the signposted Ardudwy Way up alongside the wall – *enjoying new mountain views, including Snowdon.* After an old iron gate continue ahead with the path near the wall, soon

Ffynnon Enddwyn

rising past its corner and on to another gate. The path continues across the hillside above the wall towards distant Snowdon, soon descending to a waymark post by a wall. Continue down the path, taking its left fork down through bracken parallel with the wall to go through a small old gateway in the wall corner to a ladder-stile ahead. A few yards beyond the wide path bends left down the slope then meanders down the hillside to a narrow upland road. Follow it right. Shortly a kissing gate on the left gives access to Ffynnon Enddwyn almost enclosed by stones. *An information board tells you that the well is named after Santes Enddwyn who was said to have been cured of a disease after bathing in it. Its apparent healing properties covered gland related illnesses, skin diseases, sore eyes and arthritis.*

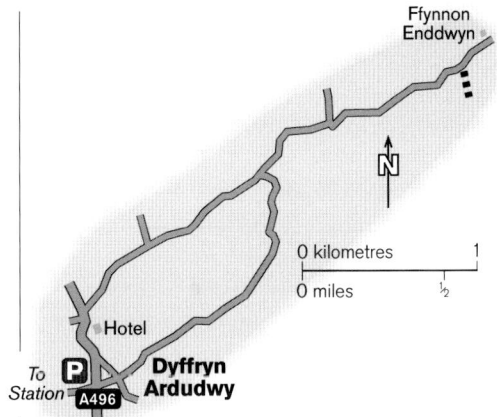

Link to Dyffryn Ardudwy

If you wish to break your journey at Dyffryn Ardudwy, when you reach the upland road, follow it westwards down past a junction, then one of two narrow roads down to the village. It is about 2¾ miles to the village centre. To rejoin the trail you can initially follow the other narrow road not used on your descent.

10 Ffynnon Enddwyn to Llanbedr

3¾ miles

The trail continues north with the Ardudwy Way, descending into the gentler landscape of Cwm Nantcol. It then leaves the Ardudwy Way and heads west down to Llanbedr through attractive countryside featuring river, lake and woodland scenery. There is the option to continue along the Ardudwy Way for ¼ mile to rejoin the trail returning from Llanbedr.

1 From Ffynnon Enddwyn continue along this scenic upland road, through a gate, past a signposted path on the left – *enjoying extensive views* – and a fenced-off mine entrance on the right. *This is the northern end of Moelfe manganese mine. It was worked in phases under various ownership from 1835 until 1917 with its peak production of over 2,500 tons in 1886 when 24 men were employed. Other subsequent years involved only a handful of underground and surface workers. Ore mined was taken down to Llanbedr station.* At a small parking area, leave the road to go through a kissing gate in the wall ahead by a finger post. Go ahead across upland pasture and down a path to a ladder-stile in the wall below – *enjoying good views into Cwm Nantcol and towards the rocky Rhinogs.* Descend to a ladder-stile/gate in the wall below then go down the next field and through a gateway in the bottom right-hand corner. Angle left down the field past the end of a farm building round to a ladder-stile. In the next field join the nearby stony access track, which you follow down to pass through a gateway. Just before a house (Penisarcwm) follow the waymarked permissive path down the field edge to a ladder-stile/gate by a small stone building and down to a finger post on the road below. Follow it left past Penisarcwm's driveway and on to cross over the Afon Cwmnantcol. At a junction with a no through road turn left down the road and on past Gelliwaen.

2 About 100 yards further the Ardudwy Way turns right off the road. (For those wishing to by-pass Llanbedr follow the Ardudwy Way up the green track. Shortly at a waymark post turn left off the track and follow the waymarked path up across an area of bracken and small crags. At another waymark post keep ahead along a brief narrow green track, then alongside the wall to a large waymarked gate. Just beyond is an information board on the old drovers route. Keep ahead down the path past another information board on 'Farming the mountain' to go through a gate below at the entrance to nearby Y Fron where you join the returning route from Llanbedr. Follow the access lane/track to cross the river at Pen-y-bont.)

For Llanbedr continue along the road, shortly passing between a house and outbuildings of Cefn Cymerau Uchaf. Continue along the road overlooking a side valley and Nantcol Waterfalls campsite, soon descending. Just after a cattle grid by an access road on the right take a path on the left angling

View across Cwm Nantcol to the Rhinogs

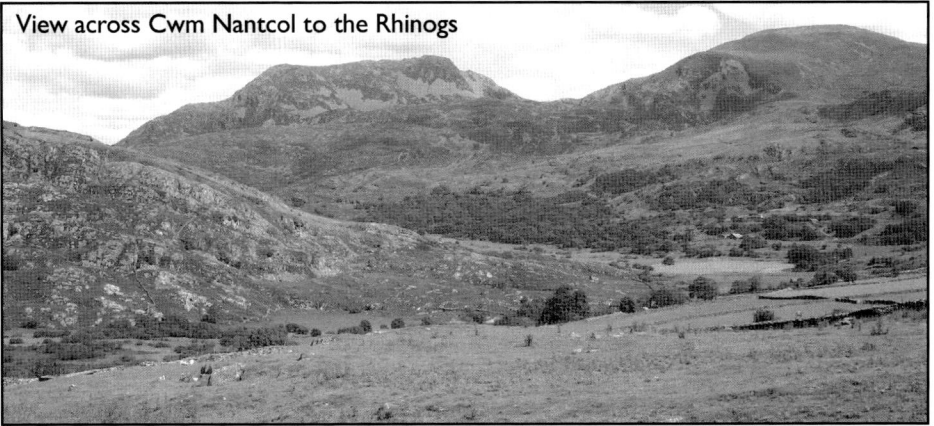

down the hillside, keeping with its right fork, to the access road for the campsite. Take a path opposite through trees to cross a footbridge over the Afon Cwmnantcol. Follow the path ahead, past an enclosed path on the left, soon passing above the river and a large reservoir to an iron gate. The wide path continues through trees to another gate, then through the mature deciduous woodland of Coed Aber Artro, owned by the Woodland Trust, to a minor road by an information board. Take the signposted path opposite down through the wood, past a path on the right, then later a wide path coming in from the left, to a gate. Just beyond turn right down a narrow access road, soon bending left past the entrance to a house. Follow the road through woodland past signposted side paths, to join another access road above the river. Just past a compound on the left take a signposted path along a track on the right to the entrance to Glan Glanffrwd Hall, then continue

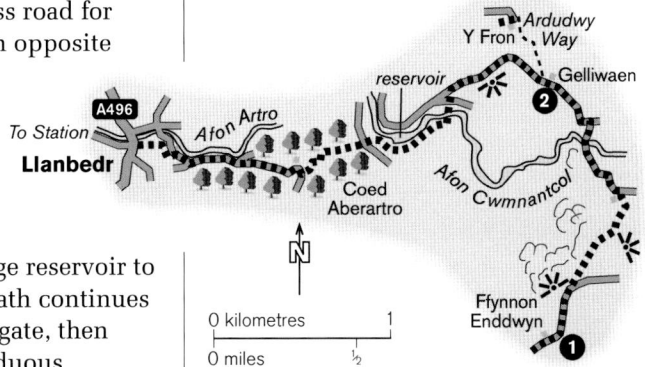

down past Tyddyn Artro cottage to go through a small metal gate. Turn right along the field edge beside the Glan Glanffrwd Hall's boundary wall. At its corner keep ahead alongside the hedge boundary to go through a small gate in its corner. Go along the edge of the football pitch and past a play area to a kissing gate by the river Artro, then to steps onto the road bridge at Llanbedr. *The small village, standing on on the coast road, developed around this important bridging point of the river. The parish became engaged in the small scale manufacture of flannel and the mining of manganese.*

LLANBEDR TO LLANDECWYN
12¾ or 11½ miles

The trail returns along another route to rejoin the Ardudwy Way, which it follows north through an increasingly remote upland area to a minor road, which offers a link down to either Llanfair or Harlech. It then continues northwards through an historic upland landscape to the remarkable Bronze Age cairn circle of Bryn Cader Faner, before beginning a long steady descent to Llyn Tecwyn Isaf, from where there are a choice of routes down to Llandecwyn and the end of the Ardudwy Way.

11 Llanbedr to the upland road near Ffridd farm
4¼ miles

The trail heads along the northern side of the Artro valley by minor roads and bridleway to visit Capel Salem, famous for one of the most iconic Welsh images ever created. It then rises through fields to rejoin the Ardudwy Way at Y Fron. From Pont Pen-y-bont it continues north along minor roads to Dinas. After passing a small attractive lake the well waymarked path then rises in stages across a hidden upland landscape of small rocky ridges and reedy areas to reach a minor upland road just beyond the remote farm of Ffridd.

▌ From the Victoria Inn follow the road signposted to Cwm Bychan/ Cwm Nantcol, shortly passing the school to leave the village. Take a signposted bridleway up an access track to Rhiw then continue up the stony track past other houses and on to rejoin the valley road. Follow it through the hamlet of Pentre Gwynfryn and on alongside the river. At a junction turn right, signposted Cwm Nantcol/Capel Salem/Nantcol waterfalls, across the bridge over the river (or you can follow the narrow road ahead signposted to Cwm Bychan direct to Pen-y-bont). At the next junction turn left signposted to Cwm Nantcol along the road beside the river, soon rising to Capel Salem. *This simple Baptist chapel, built in 1850, became famous as the location for one of the most popular paintings in the early part of the 20thC. The artist Sydney Curnow Vosper's 1908 painting of the congregation in traditional Welsh costume, entitled 'Salem', was exhibited at the Royal Academy a year later, then bought by Viscount Leverholme. It subsequently became widely known after his company, Lever Brothers, used the image to promote Sunlight soap, exchanging collectable tokens for a print of the painting, which hung in many homes, especially in Wales, where it remains highly regarded. It is said that the face of the devil can be seen in the folds of the main figure's shawl! The original painting is exhibited in the*

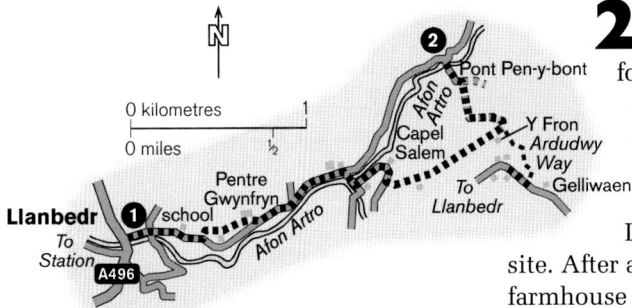

2 Go up the road ahead between cottages, then follow it to a junction. Keep ahead (Cwm Bychan), soon crossing a river. On a bend go along the no through road ahead to Dinas camping and caravan site. After a gate pass between the farmhouse and large stone outbuilding. Just beyond a pond at the gated entrance to the campsite, turn right on the path signposted to 'Lake 100 metres/Rock 1 km' to a stile/gate. The path bends up left to a gate. Follow the path ahead through bracken to reach a small attractive lilly covered lake – *a pleasant place to stop.* The next section of the Ardudwy Way to the minor road continues through a compact bracken and reed covered upland area guided by regular waymark posts. After relaxing by the lake continue on the well waymarked path, soon bending right up and across the bracken/gorse covered slope above the end of the lake, then left up across a small ridge. The path continues along the edge of a small wettish area, then bends right to a waymarked path junction. Ignore the path leading left, signposted to 'The Rock' but follow the Ardudwy Way up the bracken/heather terrain and across a shelf beneath crags to a small iron gate in the wall.

Lever Art Gallery at Port Sunlight in Cheshire. Continue up the road, past a track, then take a signposted path through a small gate on the left. The path soon rises beside a wall, then bends left up a faint narrow green track to a gate. Continue up beside the wall beneath the nearby farm. At its corner keep ahead, over a cross path, and through an old gateway in wall. Go across the sloping field and past a small wooden post by a boulder. Ignore a path angling down left, but follow a wide path rising ahead, passing just above a small information board on 'Flock management', to a kissing gate by another information board on 'A boundary gate'. Go across the field past an information board below on 'Field use' towards Y Fron. Pass below the house to join its access road. At its gated entrance you rejoin the Ardudwy Way and an ancient highway. Go down the access lane – *past a nearby information board on Coed Crafnant, a North Wales Wildlife Trust oak wood reserve* – then track to a gate. A little further at a track junction turn left and follow the track to cross the old stone bridge of Pont Pen-y-bont over the river, once crossed by drovers and stage coaches.

3 The path continues through bracken, then descends and goes along the right-hand bracken covered edge of a wet reedy area, soon bending right briefly to cross a small footbridge over a stream. The Ardudwy Way now heads left through reeds then

Lake near Dinas

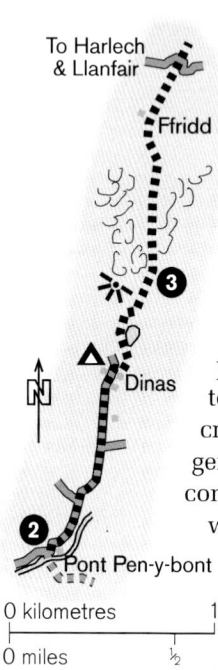

To Harlech & Llanfair

Ffridd Farm

3

Dinas

N

2

Pont Pen-y-bont

0 kilometres   1
0 miles   ½

turns right up the bracken covered, then reedy slope. Soon it bends right then angles left and rises beneath a crag and through bracken to pass through a wall gap. The path now rises to pass beneath a crag, then makes a gentler ascent before continuing to a small wooden gate in a wall. The path rises briefly again then continues to a ladder-stile by a large stone ruin. Nearby is the remote upland Ffridd farm. Go to a post ahead, then descend to a gap in a wall and continue across upland pasture grazed by sheep – *with a good view of the Rhinogs* – down to a post. Go along the left-hand edge of a reedy area,

then just before a gateway in a stone wall, bear right just below the wall and continue with the good path, passing beneath a small crag, to unexpectedly reach the bend of a narrow road.

Link to Harlech or Llanfair

If you wish to break your journey at either Harlech (2½ miles) or Llanfair (2¾ miles) turn left along the narrow scenic upland road enjoying extensive views. At a junction turn left, then at crossroads by a chapel turn right to begin a steep descent to Harlech or continue ahead on an easier descent to Llanfair.

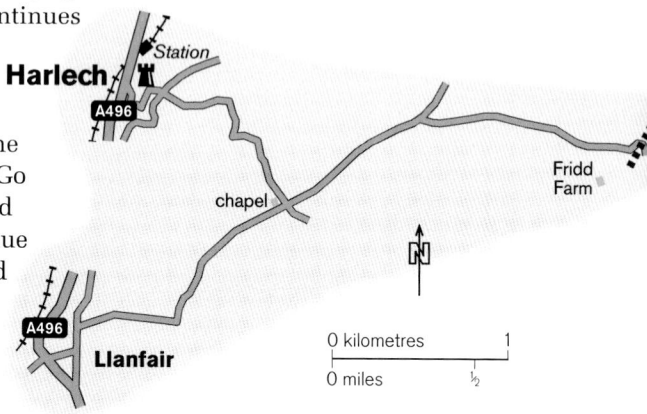

Station

Harlech
A496

chapel

N

Fridd Farm

A496

Llanfair

0 kilometres   1
0 miles   ½

12 Upland road near Ffridd farm to Bryn Cader Faner

4 miles

The trail continues northwards with the Ardudwy Way on good paths and tracks, including a Bronze Age trackway, through a wild ancient upland landscape, once occupied by early settlers, offering extensive coastal and mountain views. This very enjoyable section finishes at one of the highlights of the walk – the stunning Bronze Age burial site of Bryn Cader Faner, set on a small knoll at just over 1280 ft/390 metres beneath the northern end of the Rhinog ridge.

Bryn Cader Faner

Llyn Caerwych

cairn

cairn

Llyn Eiddew-bach

0 kilometres   1

0 miles   ½

Llyn y Fedw

2

Moel y Gerddi

Rhyd yr Eirin

1

Fridd Farm

█ Follow the signposted Ardudwy Way through a gate by a small ruin and go up Rhyd yr Eirin's access track – *with a good view of the Rhinog ridge.* As it bends towards the large remote upland cottage cross a ladder-stile ahead. Angle left for a few yards then go up the left-hand edge of a reedy area. Shortly follow a faint path up to a waymark post. Keep ahead to cross the right hand edge of a wide low grassy ridge. Mid-way angle right down and across upland pasture to a ladder-stile in the wall. At a cross path just beyond turn left then immediately angle right up another path across the gorse covered slope, soon contouring across to a gap in a wall. Continue with the good path to a ladder-stile in the wall ahead. Turn left with the path, soon taking its higher right fork across rough upland pasture to a ladder-stile in a wall. Just beyond turn right along an old track. After a few yards it bends north – with a good view of the Rhinog ridge – and continues for ¼ mile to a ladder-stile/gate. *Just to the west is Moel Goedog on which is an Iron Age hillfort.* Continue with the old part stony track (a permissive route agreed between the landowner and Snowdonia National Park Authority), shortly rising and passing between walls – *offering extensive views along the Llyn peninsula, to Criccieth, and the mouth of the Dwyryd estuary, then a series of mountains leading to Snowdon.* After another gate the track briefly accompanies a wall on your right – *offering a good view into the wild upland valley* – then makes a long steady descent to another ladder-stile/gate. It now bends right towards the ridge.

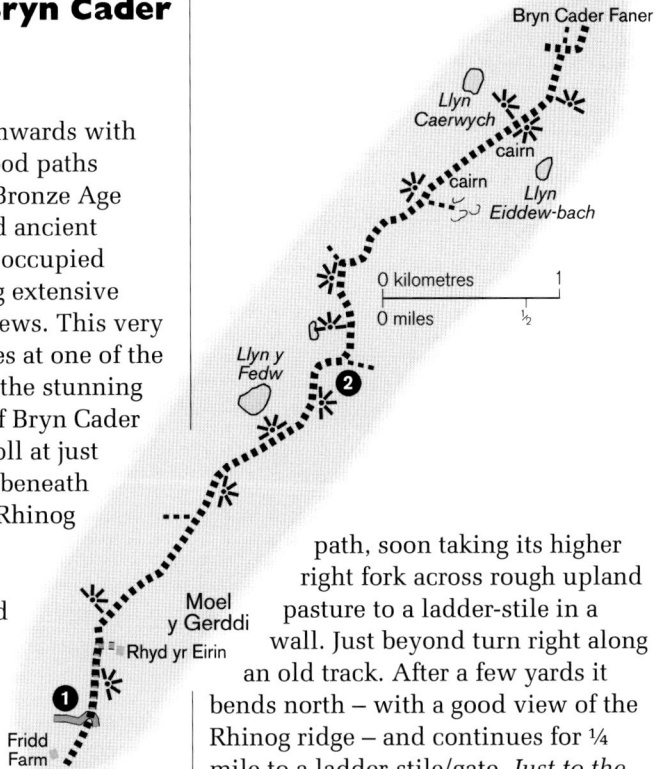

57

Bryn Cader Faner

2 Shortly, at a waymark post, you leave the track by taking a permissive path on the left. The wide path heads north across upland pasture, shortly angling right and descending – *with Snowdon ahead* – to join a wall. Follow a path a few yards above it to a ladder-stile/gate. Continue with the wide path, bending half-right to a post then descending – *with new views* – to join another old part stony track. Follow it right, shortly rising to a ladder-stile/gate, then to another ladder-stile/gate ahead. Continue with the now delightful narrow green track across the wild treeless upland landscape. Shortly take a waymarked path on the left at a good viewpoint looking west along the Llyn peninsula. The path follows the wall on the left, soon rising, then widens as it angles away from it to go over a small rise. The wide path now continues unerringly straight across rough upland pasture near the northern end of the Rhinog ridge, passing close to ancient cairns. *You are now walking along a section of a Bronze Age trackway from Llanbedr to Trawsfynydd and onwards to Bala.* It fades as it crosses a short wet reedy area then continues its course. *To your right you will see the continuing previous track and Llyn Eiddew-bach.*

The path then bends more north – *with a view ahead of Bryn Cader Faner. On higher ground to your left are the remains of ancient hut circles.* After another short wettish reedy area you rejoin a good path. At a waymark post at a crossroad of paths where the Ardudwy Way turns left, first turn right and follow a path up to visit Bryn Cader Faner – *a great place to stop to enjoy panoramic mountain views and to savour the splendid upland landscape which you will shortly be leaving.*

Bryn Cader Faner is one of the finest Bronze Age sites in Wales. This impressive small cairn circle, 28 feet wide and about 3 feet high is edged by 15 thin stone slabs of up to 6 ft in length set at an angle like a crown of thorns. It is thought that originally there were about 30 slabs. Some on the east side were removed by the army before World War II when incredibly the cairn was used as a target during gunnery practice. The hole in the centre, which once contained a cist or grave, was caused by treasure hunters in the 19thC. The cairn's design and dramatic setting was clearly chosen to impress travellers heading north along the ancient trackway which passes beneath it.

13 Bryn Cader Faner to Llandecwyn

4½ or 3¼ miles

The trail now begins a long steady descent from the wild upland landscape on paths and minor roads following the Ardudwy Way to the attractive lake of Llyn Tecwyn Isaf, enjoying extensive views on the way. Afterwards there is a choice of routes to Llandecwyn. You can continue with the final section of the Ardudwy Way by minor upland road and ancient track past Llandecwyn's old remote parish church to the large scenic reservoir of Llyn Tecwyn Uchaf, then down a wide path in a side valley to Llandecwyn (Route A). This is the recommended route if you are not continuing with the trail to Porthmadog. Alternatively, you can take a more direct descent route on a path featuring a superb viewpoint (Route B) or on a scenic minor road, offering similar views (Route C). It is an additional ⅓ mile down the Porthmadog road to Llandecwyn station.

I Return down to the waymark post at the crossroad of paths and continue ahead on the Ardudwy Way across a reedy area to rejoin the wide path, which improves as it rises and meanders across the hillside before beginning a long descent – *with good mountain and valley views* – to a waymark post, where it bends left and continues across the right-hand edge of a large flat reedy area. At a second post it bends to cross two low footbridges

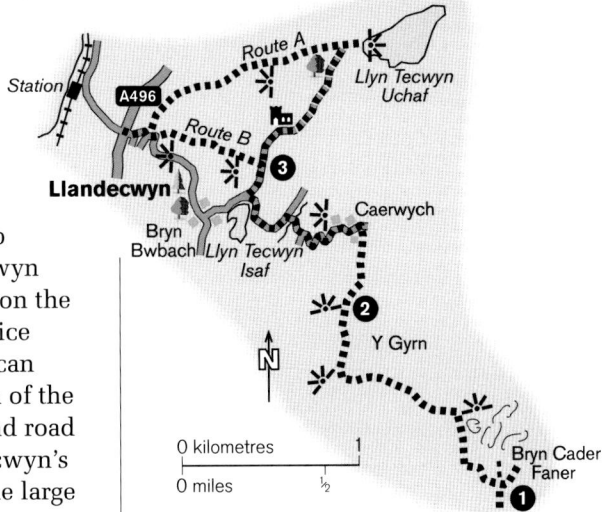

and continues to a further post. The wide path now descends towards the Dwyryd estuary to a post. Here bend right down to another post, then angle right across the stream to join a path a few yards beyond reeds. It continues at the bottom of a slope beneath craggy Gyrn, then makes an inclined descent – *with views across the Dwyryd estuary to Portmeirion and Porthmadog beyond, and along the Llyn peninsula* – to a gate. The path continues on a steady descent – *with a view of Llyn Tecwyn Isaf* – to pass through an old gateway in a wall.

2 Ignore a path bending right but continue ahead along the right hand side of a reedy area, soon joining a wide path which descends to a waymarked old gateway in a wall. Ahead can be seen a glimpse of Llyn Tecwyn Uchaf. Continue down the rougher path, through a waymarked

59

gateway and on with the occasionally faint and narrowing green track, soon descending to pass through a gateway. As it bends away from the wall keep ahead briefly near the wall to follow another faint narrow green track down to a minor road by a farm. Follow it left down past Caerwych Riding Centre. The road then meanders down the hillside to a gate onto another road. Turn right down the road and over the river. At a junction turn left up the road, then follow it alongside Llyn Tecwyn Isaf. *This beautiful lake, partly edged by water-lilies, is home to a variety of dragonflies, some rare in Wales.* Just before the road meets another angle right up to a nearby waymark post then turn right up the other road. (For Route C follow the road further along the lake then at the next junction in Bryn Bwbach by Capel Brontecwyn turn right and follow the narrow scenic road down to the A496 in Llandecwyn.) Follow the road up to a signposted cross-path by a barn.

3 Here you have a choice.

Route A

Continue up the road to its end at a cottage and nearby St Tecwyn's church. *This small remote church, mainly dating from 1879-80, replaced an earlier medieval church which is said to have stood on the site of an even earlier 6thC Celtic church. It was sited at a great viewpoint adjoining an ancient highway, possibly Neolithic in origin, that was once the main road to Mentwrog. For centuries the church served the original scattered upland parish of Llandecwyn.* Continue along a track designated unsuitable for motors to a gate. This ancient highway rises steadily, then descends to pass under power cables, where you join a waymarked section of the Wales Coast Path near hidden Llyn Tecwyn Uchaf. The Ardudwy Way now bends left with it, but first go to a waymarked gate ahead, then along a wide path to the dam of the reservoir – *which makes a good place to stop before your final descent to Llandecwyn.* Retrace your steps, then follow the waymarked Ardudwy Way, now shared with the Coast Path, down to a gate, then to a ladder-stile/gate. The path continues down the attractive narrow valley – *somewhat spoilt by pylons.* Later go past a gate in a wall on your right and continue ahead up the path alongside the wall to a waymarked gate by a building. Go past the house to a road in Llandecwyn and follow it down to the A496 and the end of the Ardudwy Way.

Route B

Cross the large stone stile by the finger post and go across the large field to a ladder-stile in the wall ahead – *enjoying extensive views.* Keep ahead down the next field to another ladder-stile, then descend through trees to a step stile below. Continue to a gate in the boundary ahead. Go up a faint green track for a few yards. (Do not be tempted to follow it further to a gate in the wall ahead, with a ruin beyond.) Instead work your way half-left through bracken and across a low ridge towards a visible cottage to go through

Llyn Tecwyn Uchaf

a small wooden gate in a wall. Join a green track just beyond and follow it left past the outbuilding of the cottage to a gate, then to another at the entrance Cynefin. Go down its access track, then just before an outbuilding and dwellings, do a sharp U-turn right up to cross a nearby stile in the fence below a telegraph pole. Follow the path through gorse to pass behind the old house, through a small gateway in the wall and past the gable end of the nearby cottage to a commanding viewpoint. *Harlech Castle is visible to the south. There are good views across the Dwyryd estuary to Portmeirion,* *and the distinctive hill of Moel-y-Gest overlooking Porthmadog, to the Llyn Peninsula and Penrhyndeudraeth. There is also a fine panorama of mountains, including Snowdon.* A path now descends beside the wall to a stile, then down through trees. At the wall corner turn left down to cross the remains of an old wall. Turn right down the field edge, soon joining another old wall which you follow down beneath tree-covered higher ground to a small gate, then kissing gate onto the minor road descending from Bryn Bwbach. Follow it down to the A496 in Llandecwyn.

LLANDECWYN TO PORTHMADOG
15½ miles

The next section of the trail follows the new waymarked Wales Coast Path on a meandering inland route around the wooded Cwm Dwyryd to Penrhyndeudraeth then continues via Portmeirion to Porthmadog, situated on the Glaslyn estuary on the edge of both the Snowdonia National Park and the Llyn Peninsula. It passes through an interesting varied landscape of woodland, upland pasture, lakes and farmland, offering changing views and close encounters with steam trains on the narrow gauge Ffestiniog Railway.

14 Llandecwyn to Tan-y-bwlch
5¾ miles

1 This section starts from the junction of the Porthmadog toll road with the A496. If arriving by train, from Llandecwyn station follow the adjoining road up to the junction, an additional ⅓ mile. From the junction go up the minor road opposite by Bryn Moel on the signposted Wales Coast Path/Ardudwy Way past a postbox and community notice board. When the road bends right take the signposted Coast Path past the side of Beudy Cil and down to a gate by an outbuilding. Follow the path down beneath the bracken-covered slope, shortly levelling out. The wide path then bends east to follow large pylons up the attractive side valley beneath

craggy Allt-galch. After a ladder-stile/gate the path continues up to a gate, then up a short section of green track to level out at a cross track. Here the Ardudwy Way begins its journey south. Turn left along the track to a nearby waymarked gate, then follow the green track to the main dam of nearby hidden Llyn Tecwyn Uchaf reservoir.

2 Follow a path above the northern side of the large lake beneath crags, passing through a small gate. At the corner of the lake the path rises gently away then follows the perimeter wall of a forest to a waymarked gate. At a stony forestry track beyond follow it left through Coed Felinrhyd. At the bend of another track go down its right fork on the waymarked Coast Path. Later, after the track bends right take a waymarked path angling down on the left. Follow the old narrow part green track meandering down through trees to go through gates on the left opposite a kissing gate, then descend to an information board on Coed Felinrhyd just above the Afon Prysor which flows from Llyn Trawsfynydd down the steep wooded Ceunant Lennyrch valley. *Opposite is Maentwrog Hydroelectric Power Station which opened in 1928. Water from the river is diverted through a pipeline down to drive turbines which generate up to 30 megawatts* of electricity, before being discharged back into the river here. From here you can follow a waymarked undulating trail clockwise around the attractive deciduous woodland, owned by the Woodland Trust. *Originally part of the large Tan-y-bwlch estate, the original oak woodland of Coed Felinrhyd was a very important source of timber for pit props used in nearby Blaenau Ffestiniog slate mines, for shipbuilding at Porthmadog, and for producing charcoal, used extensively to fuel furnaces in iron, steel and glass industries. Bark was also used in the leather local tanning industry. Timber production later intensified with the planting of faster growing conifers, but with careful management by the Woodland Trust this area of the forest has seen a regeneration of the oak woodland, along with birch, ash and hazel. The woodland trail rises in stages along the narrow attractive wooded valley to a viewing point overlooking Rhaeadr Ddu (Black Falls). After rising again, it follows a delightful track to Cae'n y Coed Bach, then descends through woodland – past the site of the murder of Williams Evans, a government tax collector – to the kissing gate just passed.*

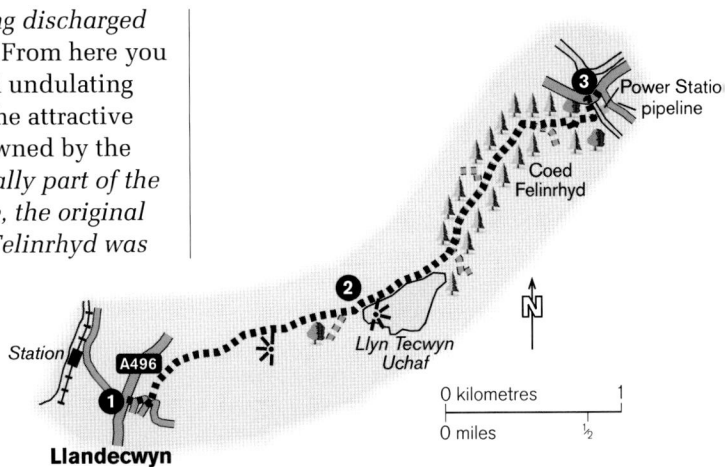

3 At the nearby A496 turn right with care across the bridge over the river, past the entrance to Magnox, then turn right up a side road on the waymarked Coast Path. The road crosses huge water pipes, then passes Bryn Derw and Felen Rhyd Fach.

After a gate the road passes through mixed woodland then continues up to another gate by an informal parking area into more open countryside. Continue up the road, shortly passing beneath crags – *with good views to the northern Rhinogs.* The road crosses a pipeline by Tyn-y-Coed and continues to rise. After a further ¼ mile turn left on the signposted path along a green track to a ladder-stile/gate. Just beyond angle left up across bracken covered ground to a waymark post, with a large pylon straight ahead. Here turn left along the edge of a reedy area, then angle right across a sleeper bridge over a wettish area. Bear left along the field edge – *with good mountain views* – to pass just to the right of a small stone ruin to a gap in a wall by a waymark post. Descend steps.

4 The way ahead is across the small reedy area below and through the middle of a small gorse covered ridge just beyond, but it is easier to go round the ridge's right hand end. Continue across open pasture

63

towards the Moelwyns, passing under power cables about 15 yards below a telegraph pole to your right, to go through a large gap in the wall ahead by a waymark post. Follow a path ahead just to the right of a small bracken covered ridge, then down across upland pasture – *with a view down to Tan-y-bwlch.* When the path fades angle right down to go through a gap in the wall near the bottom field corner by a waymark post. Angle left then follow the field edge round to a ladder-stile in the fence. Go down the path beside an old wall through trees to a rough stony track and follow it right. Just before a large stone barn turn left for a few yards then head half left to pass a large tree and cross the end of a small ridge to a waymark post beyond. Go down the part bracken covered slope to the boundary wall corner of the nearby house, then descend the edge of the large field beside the wood to a small iron gate in the corner. Descend steps, then join the nearby track which you follow right, down to a gate onto a road. Follow it down into Maentwrog. At the junction with the A496 turn right through the village past The Grapes Hotel, a 17thC coaching inn. *Maentwrog, a small village straddling the A496, lies at the highest navigable point of the Afon Dwyryd and at an important crossing point linked to several strategic routes, including the Roman Road of Sarn Helen. Maentwrog is mentioned in the Mabinogion, a collection of stories taken from medieval Welsh manuscripts, and other records indicate that there was a hostelry here in the late 13thC. The village*

church is dedicated to Twrog, a 6thC saint . Outside the church is a large stone that according to legend a giant named Twrog threw down into the settlement, destroying a pagan altar. The present village was built as an estate village in the early 19thC by the wealthy Oakley family who lived in Plas Tan y Bwlch on the opposite side of the valley. It contained a school for about 80 children, additional places of worship for Independents, Calvinistic and Wesleyan Methodists, and had four Sunday schools. Some of its inhabitants were engaged in small scale manufacture of flannel and the knitting of stockings. At the end of the village cross the old stone bridge over the river. At the junction with the A487 turn left (Porthmadog) and walk along the roadside cycle/walkway, shortly crossing to the other side. Go over a side road, then turn right on the B4410 signposted to Rhyd to the Oakley Arms Hotel. Nearby are a bus shelter and toilets.

The grade II listed hotel is a traditional coaching inn dating from the 17thC, but largely remodelled during the 18thC when it played an important part in the local community, serving as a meeting place for local businessmen, an occasional court house and police station. It was originally known as the Tan y Bwlch Inn but from the middle of the 19thC carried the name of the Oakley family from nearby Plas Tan y Bwlch who owned the large local estate that the hotel served. Its 19thC crest means 'I'm cautious but I do not fear'. In 1910 it was sold from the estate and had a chequered history during the rest of the century. The hotel has now been restored to its former glory and

offers good hospitality for the passing traveller.

Bridge over the Afon Dwyrd, Maentwrog

15 Tan-y-bwlch to Penrhyndeudraeth
4½ miles

The trail continues with the Coast Path to Penrhyndeudraeth. It first passes through attractive woodland near Plas Tyn y Bwlch, whose gardens and house you can visit, to the small attractive lake of Llyn Mair. After crossing the Ffestiniog Railway the trail follows tracks through the forest to a small hidden reservoir, then continues on some newly created footpaths through mixed woodland to eventually accompany the railway to the outskirts of Penrhyndeudraeth.

Plas Tan y Bwlch was the country house for the large Tan y Bwlch estate that had developed during the 17th and 18thC. During the 19thC the house was rebuilt for the Oakeley family and the estate flourished under its ownership driven by wealth from its large slate quarry in Blaenau Ffestiniog until the beginning of the 20thC. Today it is the Snowdonia National Park Environmental Studies Centre, offering a variety of courses. Its gardens are open 10.00–dusk, the conservatory 10.00–16.00 Monday–Friday and most weekends, whilst the house opening varies – see details in the conservatory.

■ Just beyond the Oakley Arms Hotel follow the signposted Coast Path along the driveway to Plas Tyn y Bwlch, passing the lodge, then shortly crossing a stream. With a view of the house ahead turn sharp right on the waymarked Coast Path up a stony track through woodland, past side paths

and a waterfall, shortly above a small pool. At a track junction by post no. 11 turn left to a seat with a good view along Llyn Mair. *This artificial lake, bordered by ancient oak woodland, was created by Mary Oakley of Plas Tyn y Bwlch in the 1890s. It provided water for a hydro-electric system that generated electricity for lighting the house.* Continue with the narrow stony track briefly alongside the lake, then when it splits go through a waymarked old gateway and follow the track up through trees. When it does a sharp U-turn left go past a waymarked gateway ahead and along a wide path. Soon go up its left fork past post 8 and a side path to a stile/gate. Go along a short fenced path and across the narrow gauge Ffestiniog Railway – *heeding the warning signs* – to a ladder-stile opposite. Continue up a rough track above the railway through a predominantly conifer plantation.

The Ffestiniog Railway opened in 1836 as a horse and gravity single narrow-gauge (almost 2 ft) tramway linking developing slate quarries at Blaenau Ffestiniog with the new Port Madoc, now Porthmadog, where slate was loaded onto sea-going vessels. The line, which crossed hilly terrain, was graded so that loaded slate wagons could descend by gravity. Horses, which travelled in special wagons, then pulled the empty wagons back. In 1863 small purpose built steam locomotives were introduced on the line in response to the high slate traffic demands. A year later the railway was allowed to carry passengers. In subsequent decades slate traffic on the

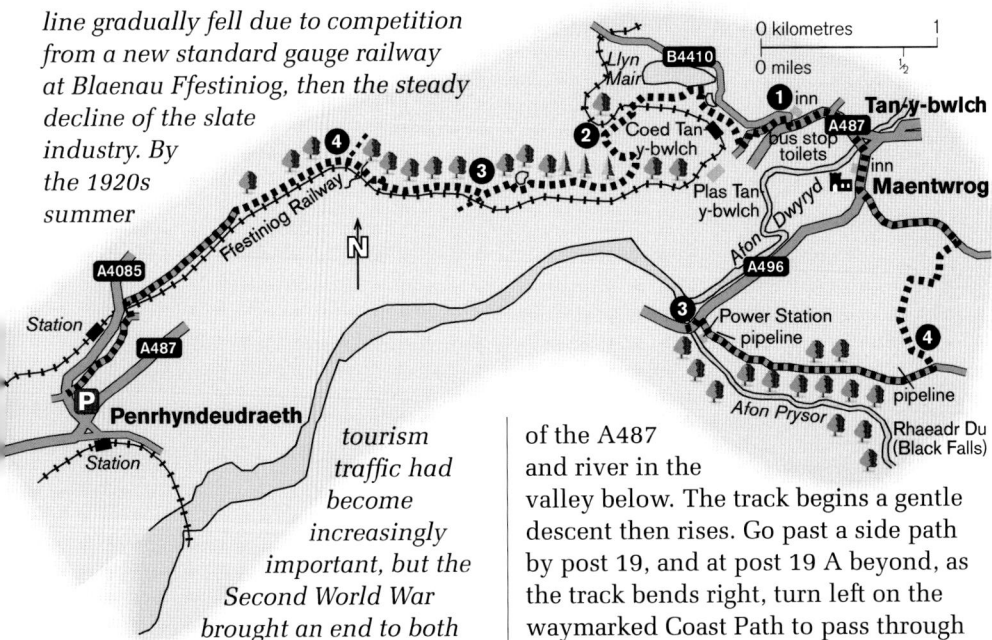

line gradually fell due to competition from a new standard gauge railway at Blaenau Ffestiniog, then the steady decline of the slate industry. By the 1920s summer

tourism traffic had become increasingly important, but the Second World War brought an end to both slate and passenger traffic, resulting in the line closing in 1946. However in the 1950s a charitable Trust was established with the aim of rebuilding the line. Restoration work began at Porthmadog followed by years of mainly voluntary labour and the overcoming of numerous obstacles. One of the greatest challenges was to build a large spiral of new track just to the east of here at Dduallt to enable the railway to gain height to by-pass a new reservoir which had submerged the original trackbed. Finally, in 1983 the 13½ mile narrow gauge heritage railway reopened and now carries thousands of visitors each year.

2 At a track junction by post 7 turn left on the waymarked Coast Path past an area of cleared trees. When it splits at post 6 take the right fork, soon bending right with glimpses

of the A487 and river in the valley below. The track begins a gentle descent then rises. Go past a side path by post 19, and at post 19 A beyond, as the track bends right, turn left on the waymarked Coast Path to pass through a gap in the wall by a small reservoir. Follow the wide undulating stony path through trees and along the end of the reservoir to cross a footbridge at post 20A onto a cross-path. Turn left and follow the narrow path down through deciduous woodland. Go past a path leading left by post 21 and follow the wider waymarked Coast Path ahead down through conifers.

3 At post 22 ignore the waymarked public footpath angling down left but continue ahead with the Coast Path along a wide level path, with the railway line below, through deciduous woodland, with glimpses through the trees of the river below. When the wide path ends follow a narrower path down through trees towards the railway line, then rising again. Shortly the path descends and bends right down through trees to pass through a

67

wall. The path continues down beside the wall and on through trees, shortly bending right then left down to a footbridge over a stream. Just beyond, the path bears left and rises through trees, with the substantial stone embankment supporting the railway nearby. The wide path bends away from it then turns to continue parallel with the railway 15 yards away. At post 39 with a green track leading right, turn left on the Coast Path.

4 At a gated crossing of the railway the Coast Path turns right and continues beside the wall adjoining the railway. At a telegraph pole the waymarked path angles right a few yards up through trees then continues along the edge of the wood to a stone stile. The path continues beside the wall, past a railway signal and nearby Rhiw Goch railway box, then moves a little way from the line – *offering a good view across the valley to the Rhinogs and the estuary* – before continuing parallel with it through an area of small trees. At a second waymark post the path bends right, then just before another post it bends left past further posts to reach a kissing gate. The path crosses a more open area, containing some young deciduous trees, to join a green track. Follow it left to pass through a gate in a wall at a signposted path/bridleway junction. Go along the track past barns and through the waymarked gate ahead. Continue along nearby Rhiw Goch's access lane to eventually reach the A4085 at the outskirts of Penrhyndeudraeth. Turn left a few yards then just before the village

sign do a sharp U-turn left to follow the signposted path down steps and under the railway. Follow the wide part stepped path down past houses, then turn left down a rough road. At a junction turn right and follow the road to a junction with the A4085 by a car park and toilets in the centre of Penrhyndeudraeth.

Penrhyndeudraeth stands on a peninsula between the estuaries of the Afon Glaslyn and the Afon Dwyryd. In the early 19thC the small community here was engaged in fishing and cockling, and was known locally as 'Cockletown'. The present village was created from the 1850s on land reclaimed from the marshes and the draining of a lake that occupied where the centre of the village is today. In 1865 its growth was boosted by the arrival of the railway and in 1872 by the establishment of an explosives factory on the outskirts of the village producing gun cotton. Thus began a long association between Penrhyndeudraeth and the manufacturing of explosives. A few years after an explosion destroyed the first works in 1915, the site was developed by Cooke's Explosives Ltd and later ICI, producing millions of munitions for war and explosives for quarrying and mining. The decline of the coal mining industry in the 1980s led to the closure of the factory in 1995. The village has two stations, one of the mainline Cambrian Coast railway and the other on the narrow gauge Ffestiniog Railway. It is home to Snowdonia National Park Authority headquarters.

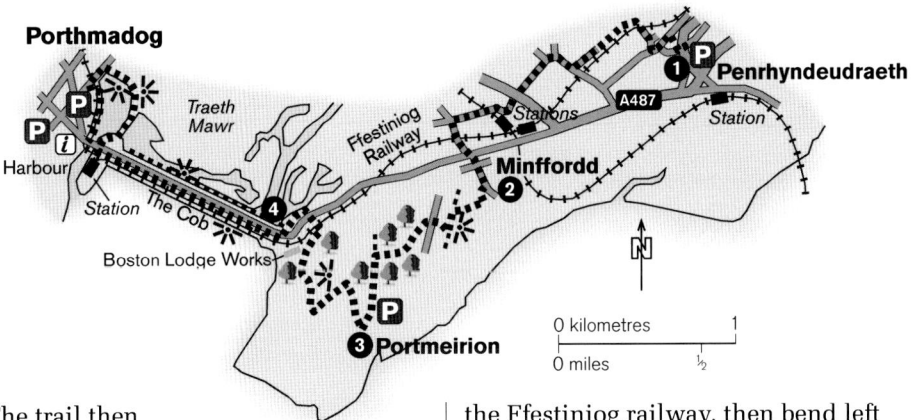

16 Penrhyndeudraeth to Porthmadog

5¼ miles

The trail now continues west via quiet roads and a path near the Ffestiniog Railway to Minffordd where it rejoins the Coast Path, which currently goes along the A487. It then follows several bridleways, passing very close to Portmeirion, the famous Italian style village designed and built by renowned architect Sir Clough Williams-Ellis and now a major visitor attraction in North Wales. A short link path connects to this unique coastal village, which is well worth a visit. (There is an admission charge, but reduced tickets can be booked in advance via www.portmeirion-village.com).

of Traeth Mawr, the upper former Glaslyn estuary. The preferred route is to walk along the top of The Cob itself alongside the railway, which offers stunning views and close encounters with steam trains. On entering Porthmadog the trail makes a short attractive and peaceful loop via Ynys Tywyn and tidal gates around both sides of the tidal basin to finish by the harbour.

❚ From the large car park and toilets in Penrhyndeudraeth cross the adjoining A4085 and go along Pensarn opposite, then take a signposted enclosed path on the right up to another road above. Follow it left past the junction with Pensarn then go up the next narrow road on the right. Follow its left fork up to pass under

The trail then meanders north to Boston Lodge Halt on the Ffestiniog Railway before heading on a choice of parallel routes across The Cob, an early 19thC feat of engineering, into Porthmadog. The Coast Path follows a wide surfaced cycle/walkway below the road, offering more intimate views

the Ffestiniog railway, then bend left along the stony track on a signposted path. At a finger post, where the concrete track bends right, go to a small wooden gate ahead. Follow the path beside the railway to steps and a stile and on briefly above the railway. Continue along the right-hand side of the long field to a small

69

wooden gate onto a lane by houses. Turn left and follow the access lane beneath the railway line, then turn right along a minor road. Follow it past two no through roads, under a large road bridge, past a farm and over the main railway line. At crossroads by houses turn left up the road, over the Ffestiniog railway line, to reach the main road at Minffordd. Use the nearby Pelican crossing to reach the road opposite, where you rejoin the signposted Coast Path. Go along the road past the entrance driveway to Portmeirion and a signposted bridleway, then continue ahead along the minor road.

2 Just below Wenydd B&B turn right on the signposted bridleway/Coast Path through a gate into a field. Go along a green track then just before a gate turn right and follow the Coast Path up the field edge to a small gate in the corner at a signposted bridleway junction. Turn left along the track – *enjoying extensive views along the estuary and to the Rhinogs.* At another signposted bridleway junction by a house turn right up an access lane. Cross Portmeirion's driveway and go up the signposted bridleway opposite through trees to an old iron gate into a field. Go up the edge of the large field, through a gateway and past outbuildings to a signposted crossroad of bridleways. Turn left along a green track to Plas Canol, then go through the bridle gate ahead. Continue down the right-hand side of the large field – *with the car park to Portmeirion visible below* – to a small gate in the corner amongst trees. Here a path

leads left to the car park If you wish to visit Portmeirion. Continue ahead down to where you have a glimpse of Portmeirion.

Portmeirion was built alongside the Dwyryd estuary by Sir Clough Williams-Ellis in two stages between 1925-1976. This compact Italian style village has attracted famous visitors over the years and been used as the location for many films. It is perhaps best known as the setting for the classic 1960s TV series 'The Prisoner'. Portmeirion is now owned by a charitable trust and caters for residential and day visitors, as well as weddings.

3 Here the bridleway does a U-turn right and rises through trees to a large iron gate. Go through the wall gap ahead and up through a small clearing to a large wooden gate and an old stone gateway. Continue near the wall past woodland to another signposted crossroad of bridleways. Turn left with the Coast Path along the part stony track. When it bends left towards the farm keep ahead to a waymarked gate by outbuildings – *with a good view of The Cob leading to Porthmadog and the coast beyond.* Go along the field edge and in the corner turn right past a gate at another good viewpoint. When the boundary bends left keep ahead across the field towards the far corner then bend left to go through a waymarked gate. Continue with the Coast Path, soon passing along the top edge of a steep wooded slope, then descending to a large gate. Continue with the bridleway down

Train leaving Porthmadog

through woodland, shortly joined by another, to a waymarked gate at Boston Lodge Halt Crossing on the Ffestiniog railway. At the other side turn left then follow a stony track down to the main road. Cross with care to the pavement opposite and follow it left to join cycle route 8 shared with the Coast Path. After passing under an archway, a kissing gate on the right gives access to a nearby bird hide in Traeth Glaslyn Nature Reserve. *The North Wales Wildlife Trust owned Reserve, at the edge of the Glaslyn estuary, includes open water, mudflats, marshes, wet*

grassland and alder woodland – a range of habitats that support a variety of birds and plants. Go past information boards on Porthmadog and Y Cob. *Nearby Boston Lodge Works at the eastern end of The Cob has been the main workshops of the Ffestiniog Railway since 1847. Originally the site provided workshops, stables and barracks during the building of The Cob and also stone from a quarry for the embankment itself. Boston Lodge was named after Boston in Lincolnshire where Maddocks was an MP.*

71

4 You now have a choice of routes into Porthmadog. The Coast Path follows the wide surfaced cycle/walkway below the road and across the former estuary close by the channel of the river. A more interesting alternative is to access the adjoining pavement, cross the road with care and take a signposted path up steps opposite onto The Cob. Follow the path along embankment beside the narrow gauge railway, enjoying if timed right, close views of a steam locomotive pulled train passing by. *Just to the south across the saltmarsh the Glasfryn estuary meets that of the Dwyryd at Traeth Bach. To the north Traeth Mawr, much of its saltmarsh reclaimed, extends towards a panorama of mountains, including Snowdon, Cnicht and the Moelwyns. As you near Porthmadog overlooked by craggy Moel-y-Gest, you will see alongside the main channel of the Afon Glaslyn near the harbour the small island of Ceri Ballast – so named because it was formed from the dumping of ballast from slate carrying ships returning to Porthmadog.*

The Cob

For centuries crossing the wide upper Glasfryn estuary, known as Traeth Mawr, was dangerous because of the strong tides or soft sands. Since the 16th C there had been talk about attempting to reclaim Traeth Mawr but only small-scale works took place. It was left to William Maddocks (1774-1828) to have the necessary vision, commitment and financial resources to tame it. Descended from a noble Welsh family he was born in London, educated at Oxford, and was twice an MP in England. He later acquired land in the area and built the small town of Tremadog on reclaimed saltmarsh.

His ambitious proposal for a stone embankment across the mouth of the estuary to keep out the sea received Parliamentary consent, and with it the prospect of reclaiming large sections of land from the estuary marshes. Hundreds of men were involved in the mammoth task, starting from both ends, and an old ship full of rocks was sunk to bridge the gap between them. Finally, after several years of endeavour and at a cost of £160,000 – a considerable amount of money in those days – on 11th September 1811 the one mile long embankment, known as The Cob, with a toll road, was opened, with due celebration.

Unfortunately early the following year the embankment was breached by the sea. After necessary repair work it reopened in 1814 and it has stood the test of time for two hundred hundred years, surviving further severe storm damage on occasions. The building of the embankment caused the diversion of the channel of the Afon Glaslyn and altered forever the nature of the hitherto large upper estuary, Treath Mawr, large parts of which were reclaimed for agricultural land.

Just past the Ffestiniog Railway station cross the road to Cob Records and turn left then right signposted to Ynys Tywyn. Go past a rising stepped path and over a slate stile, then follow the path above the river beneath the tree covered knoll of Ynys Tywyn – *once a small island before The Cob was built.* When it splits first take the left fork down to a seat at the water's edge for mountain views, then continue up the other path and around the edge of Ynys Tywyn, past a stepped path on the right, to reach an open area. Angle left to join an enclosed path passing the Environment Agency's controlled tidal gates. *These gates regulate the tidal flow of the Afon Glaslyn, closing about 2 hours before and 3 hours after high water.* Continue along the wide surfaced walkway between Llyn Bach – *created as a flood control pool for the harbour when it was built* – and the water of Traeth Mawr. *Seats make a good place to stop to look back at The Cob, Rhinog ridges, and coast stretching down to Harlech.* Continue along the walkway, then at its end bear left along the pavement. After crossing the narrow gauge railway turn left along a signposted fenced path, then cross the railway line into the nearby delightful grass recreational area with picnic tables. Walk along its edge overlooking the estuary, later joining a wide surfaced path beside the narrow gauge railway, then crossing it to join the main road by Pont Britannia. Cross to the Tourist Information Centre and harbour opposite.

Porthmadog

The building of The Cob led to the creation of Porthmadog as a flourishing town and seaport. Maddocks had realised that the diverted river had created a natural harbour, deep enough for ocean going sailing ships, and in 1821 an Act of Parliament gave permission for the development of a new port at that location. It opened in 1825 and became known as Port Madoc. From the beginning it served the slate quarries of the Ffestiniog area, with slate carried in small boats down the Dwyryd and transferred onto sea-going vessels. In 1836 the opening of the Ffestiniog Railway, which was laid across The Cob, enabled slate to be transported directly from the quarries to the port, which was a major boost to the slate industry. Port Madoc became a bustling port exporting slate all over the world and a town began to rapidly grow alongside it. At its peak over 1000 vessels used the harbour in any one year. There was also a thriving ship building industry and its three-masted schooners built up to 1913 to carry slate were the last wooden merchant ships to be built in the U.K. It was also a busy port for salted cod. However, following the arrival of the Cambrian Railway in 1867, which offered an alternative means of transporting slate to Britain's developing industrial towns, trade began to decline and the loss of the German slate market at the start of World War I led to the port's final demise. By 1945 the last of the slate ships had gone and a year later the Ffestiniog Railway closed.*

Today Porthmadog is an attractive historic tourist destination, with the town now uniquely the terminus of two restored historic steam-operated narrow gauge railways - the Ffestiniog Railway and the more recently opened West Highland Railway which runs to Caernarfon. Porthmadog has also become an important sailing centre.

LLANDECWYN TO LLANBEDR STATION
11¼ miles

The trail now begins the journey south back to Barmouth following the new waymarked Wales Coast Path. The trail meanders through a largely low-level coastal landscape of saltmarsh edges, tidal creeks and estuaries, impressive sand dunes, beautiful sandy beaches and enclosed farmland. This section is relatively short in mileage and the walking is generally easy, but it provides an opportunity of visiting Harlech Castle, a World Heritage Site, and its old town. It also finishes at unmanned Llanbedr railway station, from where you can catch a train for overnight accommodation, returning the next day. Alternatively you can walk ¼ mile along the road from the car park into Llanbedr to stay or catch the 38 bus elsewhere.

17 Llandecwyn to Harlech
6½ miles

The Coast Path is signposted along a lane on the southern side of the Porthmadog toll road about 120 yards below its junction with the A496 in Llandecwyn, easily reached from nearby Llandecwyn station or the village. Follow the access lane to pass Borth Las, then go through a kissing gate below another nearby house. Go along the field edge and cross a stile on the right just before the field end, then a stream. Cross with care the railway line to a stile beyond. The waymarked stiled Coast Path now continues by the fence along a flood embankment – *a defence against high Spring tides* – meandering between a watercourse and the grassy saltmarshes of Glastraeth grazed by sheep – *enjoying a good view of the foothills.* After crossing a track the embanked path continues to a kissing gate – *with a good view to Portmeirion* – passes a gate in the fence, then shortly bends inland to another kissing gate. Continue along the embankment to a stile. Ignore another stile ahead but turn right down steps and follow the fence to cross a large footbridge over the river. Beyond turn right and follow a wide path beneath the embankment, soon beside a tidal creek, to a kissing gate by an interesting old building (Ty Gwyn Ganlas) at the edge of the small community of Ynys, which means rocky tidal island. *Its gable end hatches indicate goods were lifted from boats in the creek below.* At the road beyond by terraced cottages turn right, then take the signposted Coast Path through a gate on the left. Go along the walled green track to a kissing gate. At the wall corner beyond follow the path angling left to cross a stone stile by a gate into the left of two fields. Follow the hedge/tree boundary on the right to a small gate then a path along the next field edge. After passing a kissing gate continue alongside the stone boundary wall enclosing Llanfihangely-traethau church (St Michael's on the shore) round to a kissing gate. *In the church doorway is information on this medieval church, which underwent restoration in the 19thC. In the churchyard is a narrow monolithic pillar with a 12thC inscription.*

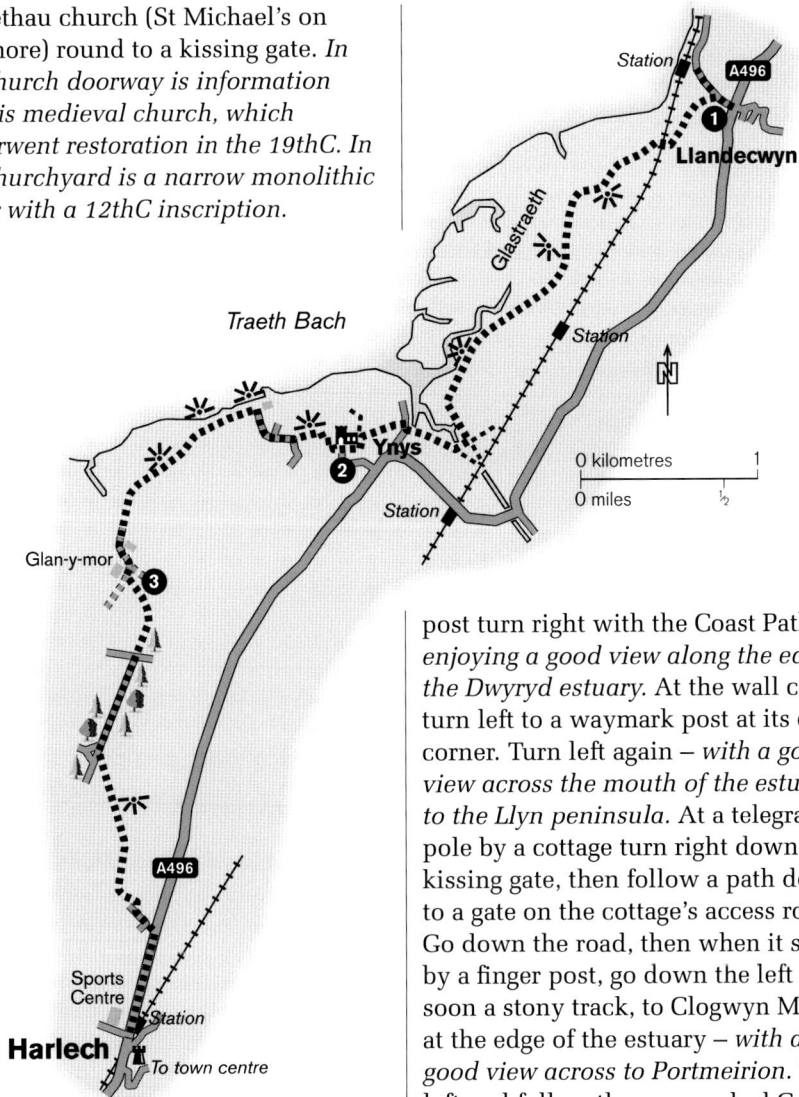

Traeth Bach

Glastraeth

Station

A496

①

Llandecwyn

Station

N

0 kilometres   1

0 miles   ½

Ynys

②

Station

Glan-y-mor

③

A496

Sports Centre

Station

Harlech

To town centre

2 Go past the church entrance to a finger post at the wall corner. Here turn right along a path, then down railed steps, across a narrow field, then up more railed steps to a kissing gate. Follow the path ahead through bracken past a waymark post. At another

post turn right with the Coast Path – *enjoying a good view along the edge of the Dwyryd estuary.* At the wall corner turn left to a waymark post at its other corner. Turn left again – *with a good view across the mouth of the estuary to the Llyn peninsula.* At a telegraph pole by a cottage turn right down to a kissing gate, then follow a path down to a gate on the cottage's access road. Go down the road, then when it splits by a finger post, go down the left fork, soon a stony track, to Clogwyn Melyn at the edge of the estuary – *with a good view across to Portmeirion.* Turn left and follow the waymarked Coast Path through trees and on parallel with the coastal hedge – *with views across the mudflats of Traeth Bach, an important feeding area for wading birds in winter, to Portmeirion and Porthmadog –* then take its right fork, soon rising above the hedge and past trees. The path, briefly sandy in nature, continues parallel with the fence to pass through a large wall gap, then angles left up through bracken to a kissing gate in the fence on your right. Turn left – *with good estuary views* – and follow the path through bracken, shortly sandy in nature, to a kissing gate beyond a stream. Go over the rise ahead, then along the base of a small bracken covered hill, shortly being joined briefly by the fence on your right. Continue to a kissing gate ahead. Just beyond angle left to pass in front of the nearby house and on to a kissing gate in the fence ahead. Join the track beyond and follow it left. At the track junction turn right to pass through the farmyard of Glan-y-mor.

3 After a large gate turn left to a nearby kissing gate, then angle right across the field to a large waymarked gate. Angle left across the next large field to join a wall, which you follow to a kissing gate in the corner. Go along the next field edge past a small conifer plantation to another kissing gate. Follow the signposted Coast Path across a nearby road to join an old unerringly straight concrete road. After ½ mile when it splits, keep ahead. At another road coming in from the right go through a kissing gate on the left. Follow the path across the large field towards Harlech Castle to a kissing gate and across the next large field to another kissing gate beyond gorse. Angle half-left across the next very large field to a waymark post by a gate in the fence. Do not go through it but continue alongside the fenced topped embanked boundary to cross a footbridge in the

corner to a kissing gate beyond. Follow the path through trees, across a large footbridge over a watercourse, through more trees and across open scrubland, then past the rear of houses. Go through a small metal gate on the right and between houses to join the nearby housing estate road, which you follow left. As it bends right go through a gap ahead to a finger post on the A496. Turn right along the grass verge, then pavement into Harlech – *enjoying ever closer views of the impressive castle on its rocky hill* – shortly passing the Sports Centre and the entrance to the railway station opposite.

The castle was built for Edward I between 1283 and 1290 by hundreds of skilled craftsmen and labourers, under the supervision of the Frenchman James of St George, one of the most renowned architects and military engineers of the time. It was one of a chain of castles built around the coast of North Wales to consolidate and demonstrate the English crown's power and control over the Welsh Princes' traditional stronghold of Gwynedd. The castle, one of the most spectacular in Britain, was built on a 200 ft high vertical rocky crag overlooking the sea. Over the centuries the sea has retreated, leaving the castle stranded nearly a mile from the current coastline. The castle, naturally protected on three sides by cliffs, consisted of two rings of walls, towers and a massive twin-towered gatehouse, was a formidable fortification and seemingly impregnable. It resisted a siege during a Welsh revolt in 1294-5, but in 1404, it was taken by Owain

Harlech Castle

Glyndŵr's forces in 1404 during his uprising against English rule. He established his court here, but in 1408 the castle was retaken by Harry of Monmouth, later Henry V.

During the War of the Roses the castle was subjected to the longest siege in British history between 1461–1468. before succumbing to the Yorkists. During the siege the inhabitants of the castle were able to receive vital supplies by boat by means of a long fortified staircase to the sea, which still exists. The heroic defence of the castle is said to have inspired the writing of the famous Welsh marching song 'Men of Harlech', popular at rugby matches today. During the English Civil War the castle, which supported King Charles I, surrendered to Oliver Cromwell's parliamentary forces in 1647 after a 9 month siege – the last Royalist castle to fall. In later years the castle attracted many artists. This stunning masterpiece of medieval fortification has survived remarkably well and is now a World Heritage Site under the care of Cadw. The castle and the old town that developed around it now attract hundreds of visitors each year.

If you wish to visit Harlech castle or the old town follow the A496 across the railway line, then go up a steep side road signposted to the town centre. Return down to the A496 and follow it right across the railway to the starting point of the next section.

77

18 Harlech to Llanbedr station

4¾ miles

The trail continues with the Coast Path to the edge of Morfa Harlech National Nature Reserve then heads south along the beach beside the dunes, which you will need to keep close to at high tide, to climb the cliffs of Allt-y-Mor, owned by the National Trust. After following the road down to Llandanwg the Coast Path goes along the edge of Y Maes, again owned by the National Trust, containing among the dunes the ancient church of St Tanwg. It continues along the edge of the Artro estuary to Pensarn station, then accompanies the river to a car park used for nearby Llanbedr station.

◾ At toilets beyond the Queen's Hotel, turn right along a road signposted to the beach, to reach a large car park at its end. Go through a kissing gate on the signposted Coast Path and follow the wide surfaced path between golf links, then up through dunes to pass an information board on Morfa Harlech National Nature Reserve. *Managed by the Snowdonia National Park Authority, Morfa Harlech is one of the most actively growing sand dune system in Britain, supporting rare plants and reptiles. The reserve extends north and includes much of the Glaslyn/Dwyryd estuary, with the sand flats and salt marsh of Traeth Bach providing an important feeding ground for overwintering wildfowl.* Follow the impressive sand dunes south along the beach, which at low tide becomes an expansive area of

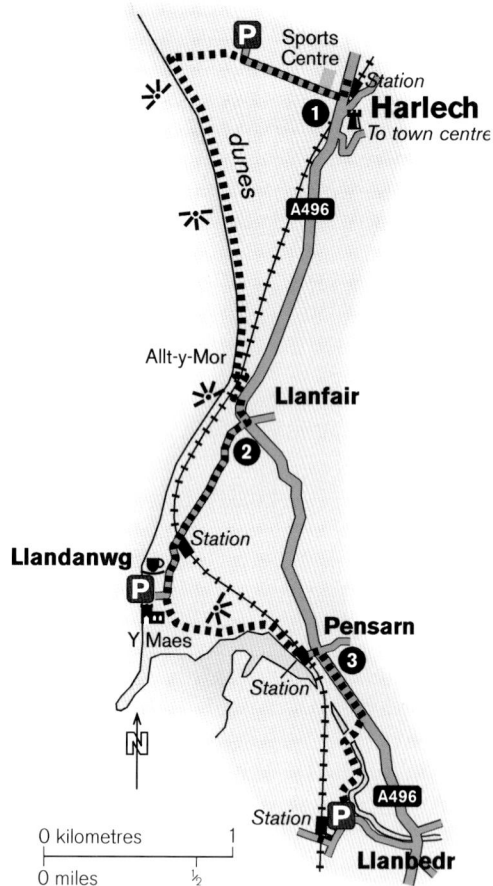

sand. At the end of the dunes continue beneath the wall supporting the railway as it passes beneath vertical cliffs, then go up steps and across the railway line. Follow the railed Coast Path zig-zagging up the vegetation covered cliffs of Allt-y-Mor, owned by the National Trust, to a small wooden gate, Turn right through trees to a nearby kissing gate and follow the wide path across the hillside up to a kissing gate onto the A496 – *with a good view looking back along the beach to Porthmadog, Criccieth and*

Artro Estuary

along the Llyn peninsula. Follow a path beside the road, then turn right down a road signposted to the railway station and beach at Llandanwg.

2 Follow the road down into Llandanwg – *with a good view to the Artro estuary and Shell Island beyond* – and over the railway line. Just before the road bends right to a car park, toilets and café adjoining the beach, go along the road ahead bending left to a kissing gate to enter Y Maes, owned by the National Trust. *Nearby among the dunes is ancient St Tanwg's church, said to have been founded in the 6thC. The present Grade I listed medieval building, dates from the 13thC. It was abandoned in 1845 and restored in 1987.* Follow the path ahead, shortly bending left above the stream, then cross it to a kissing gate. Go along a wide grass flood embankment – *with a good view ahead of the dome-shaped Moelfre and distant Rhinogs* – soon along the edge of the Artro estuary, where boats are moored, to a kissing gate. Continue along the embankment, then just before a stile and the railway line go down steps to cross a footbridge over a watercourse. Take a path angling right and continue to waymarked gates at the large house ahead near the estuary edge – *a residential outdoor centre offering watersports activities nearby.* Go past the centre, passing under arches by Pensarn harbour reception then bear left to cross the railway line at Pensarn station.

3 At the A496 turn right and follow the signposted Coast Path along the grass verge to a kissing gate, then follow the fenced path below the road to another kissing gate. Turn right and walk alongside the tree boundary of a field then go up steps on the right to cross a large black and white cast iron footbridge over the Afon Artro. Just beyond turn left along an embankment to a ladder-stile and on above the river. At the end of the embankment cross a stile and follow a path to a small wooden gate. Continue by the river then go up the slope into the adjoining car park and picnic site. At its entrance turn right along the road then follow a wide surfaced pathway below the road. At its end bend right with the road to cross the railway line at Llanbedr station.

LLANBEDR STATION TO BARMOUTH
12 miles

The trail continues with the Coast Path through one of the most scenic and popular sections of the coast. The walk south from Shell Island along the long beautiful sandy beach beneath high sand dunes is one of the trail's highlights. If conditions are favourable you may be tempted to relax awhile on the beach or treat your feet to a paddle in the sea. The Coast Path then meanders inland through enclosed farmland, visiting Tal-y-bont and later passing an ancient church before returning following the promenade into Barmouth. There are currently a few unavoidable sections of road walking, but it is hoped that over time improvement to the route will be made.

19 Llanbedr station to Tal-y-bont
7 miles

After a section of road walking (best avoided on a Saturday in the summer holidays – changeover day), then a surfaced path, the Coast Path passes through Shell Island, a very popular short break holiday and weekend destination, accessible by a tidal causeway. In the summer holidays it is packed with tents and campervans. However you soon leave the crowds behind as you enjoy 2½ miles of the glorious high sand dunes of Morfa Dyffryn National Nature Reserve and

expansive beach at low tide. You will need to keep close to the dunes at high tide. Also be aware that you pass through a designated section of beach, marked by large warning signs, where naked sunbathing and swimming are permitted. The Coast Path then leaves Benar Beach and heads by road and field paths to Tal-y-bont.

Follow the road west, later passing the former RAF Llanbedr military airfield. *This road is busy during the summer with holidaymakers travelling to and from Shell Island, so walk facing the traffic and take care. The airfield was opened in 1941 to engage German planes over the Irish Sea, with a succession of squadrons based here. After the war the airfield was used to test various new fighter jets and for the development of target drones. After its closure in 2004, there were controversial plans to reopen it as a civilian airfield. Now the site will get a new lease of life after approval was given in 2012 to reuse buildings on site for aircraft maintenance, including the dismantling of commercial airliners. Opposite the airfield is a National Air Cadets Adventure Training Centre.* Just before the bend, at the edge of the estuary, go through a gate on the left on the signposted Coast Path. Follow the wide surfaced unerringly straight raised path across a reedy area to a gate by a large airfield building. Later, at another gate in trees the surfaced path ends and you continue along a stony track. Shortly turn right along a rough road, and at a junction keep ahead through the edge of Shell Island. *In high summer you will pass tents everywhere – amongst trees, on dunes etc. – a city of tents!* When you meet a stony track on the left, with huge dunes ahead, bend right with the road. Follow it past a stony track on the left, then one on the right, shortly after which it bends up to crossroads, where the road leading left goes to a beach car park. Continue ahead along the road overlooking the main camping area – *enjoying panoramic mountain views*. At the 20 mph sign just before a road on the right do a sharp U-turn left, along a narrow road signposted to another beach car park, to enter a designated 'no camping area' with grass car parking. Follow a wide sandy path onto the beach.

A496
Station
①
Llanbedr
② Shell Island
Airfield (disused)
Morfa Dyffryn
dunes
dunes
N
0 kilometres 1
0 miles ½
Benar Beach
P
△
③
A496
△
Tal-y-bont
inn
P
Station

2 Head south along the beach past impressive sand dunes, soon leaving the crowds behind. Later you pass through a designated section of beach, marked by large warning signs, where naked sunbathing and swimming are permitted. Afterwards you pass through a popular 'textile' area – *with good views along the coast to Barmouth and beyond*. Ignore an

exit off the beach between information posts, but continue further south to Benar Beach featuring a band of pebbles below the dunes. Shortly head up across the large pebbles to a tall red and white pole carrying a life buoy and a 999 sign to leave the beach. Follow the railed wooden path through the dunes, then a track to join a road. Follow it past the Morfa

Beach by Morfa Dyffryn

Dyffryn/ Traeth Bennar car park, toilets and Benar Beach camping and touring park. Continue along the road.

3 After just over ⅓ mile take the signposted Coast Path through a small gate on the right by the entrance to Bennar Fawr. Go up the field to cross a stile into the right of two fields. Continue beside the wall, then at a telegraph pole turn right across the field to a stone stile by a larger telegraph pole. Walk through the next field towards a house to cross another stile in its left-hand corner. Turn left along the edge of the long field, shortly following the wide raised path half-right past a stone barn. Continue to other farm buildings ahead and turn right. At the waymarked wall corner turn left and follow the wall round to go through a gate by the waymarked wall end. *To the east is the domed shape of Moelfre and ahead the long ridge leading up to Diffwys.* Bear right along the field, moving away from the wall to a stile in the wall ahead. Angle right to a waymarked wall corner ahead, then bear left to go through a waymarked gate. Turn right along the field edge to a stone stile in the corner. Just beyond turn left along a track, soon near the river, to pass under the railway line. Turn left along the lane, passing between farm buildings to reach Pandy caravan park. Turn right through its entrance past reception and on along its access road past static caravans, keeping with its left fork to a gate into a field used for tourers and tents. Go up the field to a small waymarked iron gate near its right hand corner by the river into Old Mill Park. Go past log cabins, then the former corn mill with its waterwheel, and up the drive to the main road in Tal-y-bont. Cross to the village shop opposite and turn right to nearby toilets and car park.

20 Tal-y-bont to Barmouth

5 miles

The route of the Coast Path to Barmouth is currently restricted by the lack of paths near the coast. Therefore, after an initial section of field paths, there is an unavoidable 2¼ miles of walking on the pavement alongside the A496. But do not despair for you are rewarded with extensive coastal views, a pub midway and the opportunity to visit the ancient 13thC church at Llanaber. Afterwards you can enjoy a final section of delightful walking along the promenade and a fitting finish at Barmouth harbour, offering refreshments and superb views.

From the toilets cross the bridge over the Afon Ysgethin, then cross the road to the signposted Coast Path opposite. Turn right and follow the path round the cottage, then alongside the river to a kissing gate and on to a small iron gate into a field. Go down the field and through a old gateway in the wall ahead then continue along the left-hand edge of the next field to a small metal gate in the corner. Go along the access lane ahead past a house then turn right on the signposted Coast Path past the front of Aber Scethin cottage. Follow the path to a kissing gate and across the railway line to another kissing gate opposite

onto an access lane. Go through a kissing gate ahead and along a track, then turn left on the signposted path through a small metal gate into a small caravan park. Turn right along an access lane ahead. At the Play Room/ Games Room angle left to pass the reception and a shop, and follow the narrowing walled surfaced path, then stony path to a road at the entrance to Sarn Faen farm Camping and Touring site. Turn right to a nearby kissing gate and follow the Coast Path along the field edge and through a small metal gate near the corner. Go across the field to the nearer waymarked gate in the wall ahead, then along the next field edge to a stone stile. Go past the large barn and Islawrffordd farmhouse, then

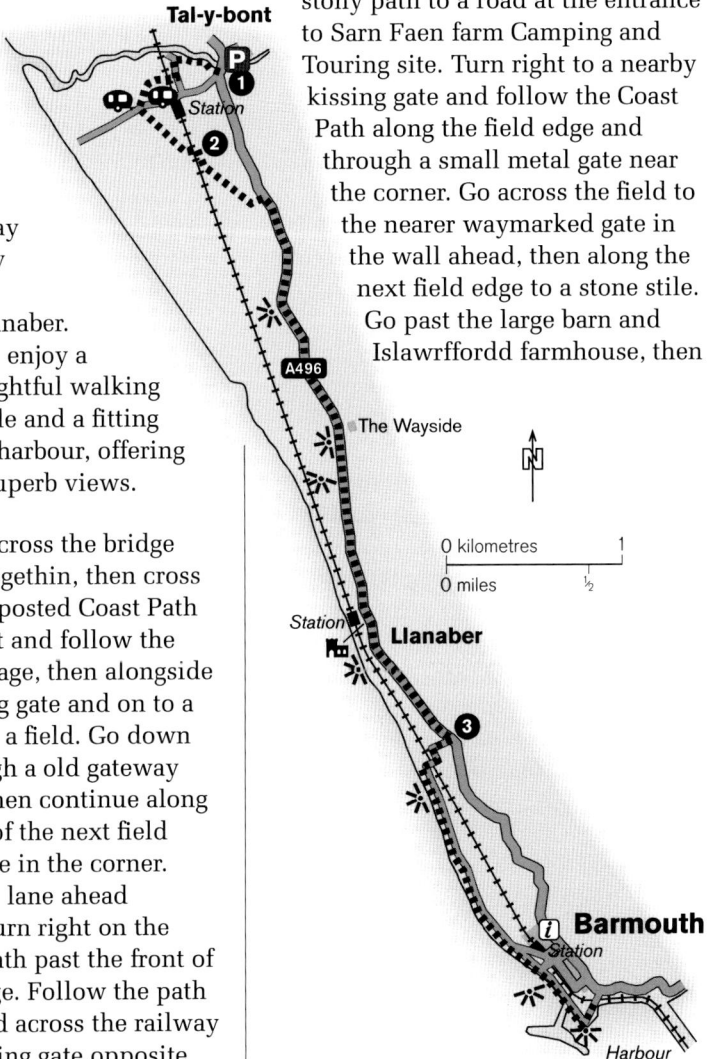

Tal-y-bont

P

① *Station*

②

A496

✳ The Wayside

N

0 kilometres ——————— 1

0 miles ———— ½

Station **Llanaber**

③

ℹ Barmouth
Station

Harbour

83

St Mary's church, Llanaber

turn left along a track to the nearby entrance to Sea Nymph Caravan Park. Turn right and keep ahead along the access lane's left fork, then a rough track past outbuildings on your left. At their end follow the green track ahead to a small metal gate to cross the railway line to another gate.

2 After crossing a stream beyond turn right to go through a waymarked gate and a nearby old gateway, then follow the Coast Path along the edge of two fields to a kissing gate. Go across the next field to cross a ladder-stile in the wall ahead and a stream below. Now head across the next field towards a house to cross a stone stile in the end of its boundary wall. Go past Y Stablau and the main house, Sebonig. When its stony access track bends up to the nearby A496 cross a stone stile ahead. Go through a small adjoining gate and up the field edge to a small metal gate onto the road by Sebonig's entrance. Continue south along the pavement past the entrance to Sunnysands caravan park and on towards Barmouth – *enjoying good views across Cardigan Bay from the Llyn Peninsula and Bardsey to the coast extending south from Barmouth.* Later you enter Llanaber passing The Wayside pub, restaurant and fish bar,

then the lane leading down to Llanaber railway station. Shortly afterwards you pass St Mary's church. *This early 13thC church built on a prominent position overlooking Cardigan Bay, stands on the site of an earlier 6thC church. It lies at the end of the strenuous 5 mile ancient upland route followed by church worshippers from Bontddu.*

3 At the entrance to Dryll-y-car turn right on the signposted Coast Path/cycle route 8 down a narrow no through lane. At the very bottom bend right along a stony track to cross the railway line to join the end of the promenade beyond. Now enjoy a leisurely stroll along the promenade above the beach into Barmouth. After passing Las Vegas Amusement a road on the left leads to the railway station and town centre. The harbour makes a better finish to the walk, so continue along the promenade past The Bath House to the dolphin water feature and on to the nearby harbour. *Enjoying the breathtaking views to the railway viaduct and Cadair Idris beyond, whilst partaking of refreshments at the harbour cafes or simply eating fish and chips al fresco, makes a superb finale for the trail.*

84

Linear walks

The generally good local public transport network allows the Mawddach-Ardudwy Trail to be undertaken as 14 linear day/half-day walks of variable length, which enables people of all ages and abilities to enjoy the long distance trail at convenience. Use the buses or trains indicated then follow the appropriate section of the Mawddach-Ardudwy Trail back to the starting point.

Bus and train services can change at any time, so please check current available services before planning any walk. (See the Transport section in Guidance Notes and Useful Information).

Walk 1 Barmouth to Dolgellau [9¾, 12¼ or 13¼ miles]
Take the X94 bus from Eldon Square in Dolgellau to Barmouth. Follow either the Mawddach Trail or the choice of main trails back to Dolgellau.

Alternative shorter walks
Arthog – Penmaenpool [8½ miles]
Park in Penmaenpool car park and take bus 28 (Lloyds Coaches) from the nearby road junction to the large lay-by beneath Arthog Village hall. Cross the main road to the grass verge opposite and follow it right, then take a signposted bridleway through two gates to reach the Mawddach Trail at point 2 in section 1 of the trail. Now follow instructions to Kings youth hostel, then either Route A or C to Penmaenpool.

Abergwynant – Dolgellau [4½, 5 or 5½ miles]
Park in Dolgellau and take bus 28 (Lloyds Coaches) to the bend by the driveway to Abergwynant farm and the minor road leading to Kings Youth Hostel. Here you can join Route C to the Mawddach Trail. Alternatively you can go up the minor road towards Kings to join Route A at Cae'n -y-Coed's rough access lane by Caban Cader Idris bunkhouse. Another option is to continue up the wooded Gwynant valley to join Route B at Kings hostel.

Walk 2 Dolgellau to Bontddu [7¼ miles]
Park at the western end of Bontddu and take the X94 bus to Eldon Square, Dolgellau. Follow instructions in sections 4 and 5 of the trail back to Bontddu. A bus stop (Hawddamor, Pont Borthwnog) at Taicynhaeaf on the A496 opposite the road to the toll bridge at Penmaenpool provides an option to break this into two shorter walks of 4½ miles and 2¾ miles respectively.

Walk 3 Bontddu to Barmouth [7½ or 6½ miles]
From Barmouth take the X94 bus to Bontddu. Go past the school and Car and Van Centre, then over the river Hirgwm to the bus stop beyond. Follow instructions in section 6 of the trail to Sylfaen, then either Route A or B in section 7 to Barmouth.

Walk 4 Barmouth to Tal-y-bont [7¼ miles]
Follow instructions in section 8 of the trail from Barmouth to above Pont Fadog, then the described link route to Tal-y-bont. Return to Barmouth by the no. 38 bus or train. Alternatively use the car park in Tal-y-bont near the village shop and catch the bus to Barmouth to start the walk.

Walk 5 Tal-y-bont to Dyffryn Ardudwy [7½ miles]
In Dyffryn Ardudwy there is a signposted car park near the junction of the road to the station and the main road. Catch the no. 38 bus to Tal-y-bont to a bus stop by toilets and car park near the village shop. From the end of the car park, turn left on a signposted path beside the wooded Afon Ysgethin, soon passing the Ysgethin Inn - a former late 19th C woollen mill. Follow the path past footbridges through the attractive woodland to a ladder-stile/gate, then continue up the wooded valley past side paths to eventually reach a lane by Lleti Lloegr - an emergency shoeing station and overnight stopping place for drovers. Turn right and follow the lane down over Pont Fadog, dating from 1762. Continue up the lane to go through a gate at its end. Continue up to a nearby track junction. Here turn left.

Now follow instructions in section 9 of the trail to Pont Scethin and on to the minor road leading to Ffynnon Enddwyn. (If you wish to visit the ancient healing well it will add an extra ½ mile to the walk.) Turn left and simply follow the scenic upland road westwards down past a junction, then either continue with this road or follow a narrower one on the left, down to Dyffryn Ardudwy.

Walk 6 Dyffryn Ardudwy to Llanbedr [6 3/4 miles]
From Llanbedr take the no. 38 bus to Dyffryn Ardudwy. There is an information board and map on the Ardudwy Way on the wall of the cafe at the junction of the main road and the road leading to the station. Either follow the signposted Ardudwy Way link route up a side road just beyond the Ael y Bryn hotel at the northern end of the village, or go up a narrower road opposite the road leading to the station. Both these scenic roads eventually

converge. Continue north eastwards and at a junction turn right. After just over a further ½ mile you are joined by the Ardudwy Way. Continue along the road to Ffynnon Enddwyn. Now follow instructions in section 10 of the trail to Llanbedr.

Walk 7 Llanbedr to Llanfair [7 miles] or Harlech [6¾ miles]
From Llanfair or Harlech take the no. 38 bus to shops near the Victoria Inn in Llanbedr. Now follow instructions in section 11 of the trail to the upland road near Ffridd farm. Turn left along the narrow scenic upland road enjoying extensive views. At a junction turn left, then at crossroads by a chapel continue ahead on a steady descent to Llanfair or turn right to begin a steeper descent to Harlech.

Walk 8 Harlech to Llandecwyn [11¾ or 10½ miles]
There is a small parking area on the left side of the Porthmadog road below the junction with the A496 in Llandecwyn. Alternatively, go up the minor road opposite the junction to find roadside parking on the right along Cilfor, or higher up at the beginning of Bryn Eithin.

From nearby Llandecwyn station take the train to Harlech station. Head south along the A496 to cross over the railway line and just beyond go up a steep road signposted to the town centre and the Ardudwy Way to reach the castle and crossroads beyond, near the Tourist Information Centre. Go up the steep road ahead past the Lion Hotel and out of Harlech into open country. After nearly a mile, at crossroads by a chapel turn left. At the next junction turn right on the signposted Ardudwy Way. The narrow scenic upland road heads east offering extensive views. After nearly a mile you reach where the Ardudwy Way crosses the bend of the road. Now follow instructions in section 12 of the trail to Bryn Cader Faner, then section 13 to Llyn Tecwyn Isaf, from where you have a choice of routes down to Llandecwyn.

Walk 9 Llandecwyn to Penrhyndeudraeth [10½ miles]
At crossroads in Penrhyndeudraeth turn along the A4085 past shops to find a large car park and toilets on the right. Return to the crossroads then go along the road opposite past The Griffin and down to the Harlech road and the railway station. Take the train to Llandecwyn station. Now follow instructions in section 14 to Tan-y-Bwlch, then section 15 to Penrhyndeudraeth. It is possible to break this down to two shorter walks to and from Tan-y-bwlch (Oakley Arms), by using both the train and the regular

1B bus service between Penrhyndeudraeth and Tan-y-bwlch during Monday-Saturday.

Walk 10 Penrhyndeudraeth to Porthmadog [5½ miles]
From Porthmadog you have a choice of bus or train options to the start at Penrhyndeudraeth: the regular bus 1B (Blaenau Ffestiniog) Monday-Saturday, alighting in the middle of village just before crossroads; the Cambrian Coast railway or the Ffestiniog Railway. Make your way to the large car park and toilets adjoining the A4085. Now follow instructions in section 16 of the trail to Portmeirion and on to Porthmadog. This walk combines well with a visit to Portmeirion.

Walk 11 Llandecwyn to Harlech [6½ miles]
Heading north on the A496 in Harlech just before the road crosses the railway line take the side road angling right (Industrial Estate) to find a small car park on the right beneath the castle. Catch the train to Llandecwyn station, then follow instructions in section 17 of the trail back to Harlech.

Walk 12 Harlech to Llanbedr station [4¾ miles]
From Llanbedr follow the road signposted to the station to find a car park on the right after ¼ mile. From its entrance turn right along the road then follow a wide surfaced pathway below the road. At its end bend right with the road to cross the railway line at Llanbedr station. Take the train to Harlech station. At the nearby A496 turn left and follow instructions in section 18 of the trail back to the car park. Alternatively, take the no. 38 bus from Llanbedr to Harlech.

Walk 13 Llanbedr station to Tal-y-bont [7¼ miles]
Use the car park by toilets near the village shop in Tal-y-bont. Go along a nearby road to Tal-y-bont station, then take the train to Llanbedr station. Alternatively, take the no. 38 bus from opposite the shop to Llanbedr, alighting at shops near the Victoria Inn. Take the road signposted to Llanbedr station. Follow instructions in section 19 of the trail back to Tal-y-bont.

Walk 14 Tal-y-bont to Barmouth [5 miles]
Take the no. 38 bus from Barmouth to the bus stop near the village shop in Tal-y-bont. Follow instructions in section 20 of the trail back to Barmouth. The alternative choice of taking the train to Tal-y-bont station involves an additional ¼ mile of road walking to the start.

Guidance Notes & Useful Information

General advice

In this guidebook I have divided the Mawddach–Ardudwy Trail into 20 short sections within seven chapters. Each section contains the detailed route descriptions, accompanying maps and notes on local history etc. On some sections of the walk I have included a choice of routes that offer different features or benefits, so you can tailor the trail according to your interests and needs.

At some point it is necessary to leave the Ardudwy Way to seek accommodation or transport down in the coastal communities. Llanbedr is my preferred choice. It breaks the Ardudwy Way into two manageable sections, whilst offering an easy and interesting descent and return to the Ardudwy Way. However, I have included described link routes to Tal-y-bont, Dyffryn Ardudwy, Llanfair and Harlech.

The maximum distance for completing all 20 sections of the trail continuously is 94 miles. If you prefer to finish the trail at Porthmadog, rather than returning to Barmouth, this makes the trail a 67½ or 70¾ mile walk.

In addition the trail can easily be broken down into separate walks:

– a 23½ – 28 mile walk around the Mawddach estuary

– a 26 – 27¼ mile walk between Barmouth and Llandecwyn following the Ardudwy Way

– a 41½ – 42¾ mile walk between Barmouth and Porthmadog following the Ardudwy Way then Coast Path

– a 49¼ – 50½ mile 'circular' walk between Barmouth and Llandecwyn following the Ardudwy Way then Coast Path

– a 23¼ mile walk between Llandecwyn to Barmouth following the Coast Path

Over ⅔ of the trail is waymarked as either the Ardudwy Way or Coast Path. The undulating part upland route around the Mawddach estuary, follows good paths and tracks. The Ardudwy Way from Barmouth to Llandecwyn is very well waymarked (buzzard silhouette on yellow background), but crosses higher upland areas exposed in bad weather and wet in places, so be well equipped and prepared. The Coast Path from Llandecwyn to Porthmadog is a meandering waymarked undulating route around the wooded Dwyryd valley. The Coast Path south from Llandecwyn to Barmouth is a low level waymarked route, using rights of way near the coast when available. Please note that the route of the Coast Path which opened in May 2012 is subject to ongoing improvements, so look out for any new signed sections.

The Ardudwy Way is supported by a web-site [www.arudwyway] and three detailed colour leaflets, covering the Northern, Central and Southern sections, available from local Tourist Information Centres.

For those wishing to undertake the trail as a continuous walk of 7 – 8 days, the daily stages will be determined as much by available accommodation on or near the trail as by level of fitness. It may be that you end a stage where you can catch a bus or train to available accommodation and return the following day to continue the trail. It is recommended though that accommodation, especially where limited or in high summer, is booked in advance.

Given the availability of public transport there is another way that the trail can be completed as a continuous walk, without carrying a full pack. From one or two accommodation bases, and by a combination of car and bus or rail, you can systematically complete each stage carrying only a day bag. Barmouth would make a good base for the walk. I would particularly recommend this approach to those people wishing to camp – a method I have used successfully to complete several long distance walks. The linear walks linked to local bus services and trains designed for day walkers, which are detailed in the previous chapter, will help in your planning.

Although undertaking sections of the trail as day walks can be undertaken throughout the year, for those planning to walk the whole trail continuously, the best time is between Spring and late Autumn. Each season offers its own appeal. In Spring the trees and hedgerows are returning to life, the woods are full of bluebells and wild garlic, and birdlife is particularly active. Summer with its long hours of daylight and sunshine allows more time to linger, especially on the beach, and enjoy the scenery. The changing colours of Autumn are especially delightful around the Mawddach estuary.

Whenever you choose to walk the trail please remember to build sufficient time into your itinerary to visit and enjoy the many places of interest along the route. Good walking boots are required along with appropriate warm and waterproof clothing to protect against the elements. Be prepared for any weather, which can vary from Spring snow on the hills to hot sunshine on the coast. The trail passes through some wild upland areas, magical on a sunny day, but more challenging in poor weather, when rain and mist can quickly descend. But do not forget the suntan cream – all day walking in the sun unprotected can cause discomfort and be harmful.

Carry plenty of drink and food, especially on those sections where facilities are limited or non-existent, as well as emergency equipment, including compass, whistle and small torch, plus an OS map. Please note that mobile phone signals can be unreliable, especially in upland areas.

Two sections of the Coast Path between Harlech and Tal-y-bont follow the seaward side of extensive sand dunes along beaches, whose expanse will vary according to the tide.

The route follows public Rights of Way or permissive paths/tracks and crosses some designated land where walkers have the legal right of access under the CRoW Act 2000.

Please remember that changes in details on the ground – ie. new stiles and gates, field boundaries, path diversions etc can occur at any time. Also be aware that the condition of paths can vary according to season and weather.

If you encounter any obstacles or other problems on rights of way please report these to Gwynedd Council Public Rights of Way (Meirionnydd area) via an online form at www.gwynedd.gov.uk or by telephoning 01341 424 507.

Maps

The route is covered by the following 1: 25000 scale Ordnance Survey maps:

Explorer Map OL18 Harlech, Porthmadog & Bala (most of the route)

Explorer Map OL23 Cadair Idris & Llyn Tegid (part of the route on the southern side of the Mawddach Estuary)

The Countryside Code

Be safe – plan ahead and follow any signs

Leave gates and property as you find them

Protect plants and animals, and take your litter home

Keep dogs under close control

Consider other people

Please observe the Countryside Code and respect any ancient site visited.

Facilities

This is a popular holiday area which is reflected in the overall good range of facilities available, but these will vary along the route. For the long distance walker the main considerations are overnight accommodation, evening meal options and refreshment stops/shops on or near the route. The internet is now a good source of information for planning your walk, along with the area's Tourist Information Centres. The following information is a guide but inevitably details will change. More information on specific named places can be found on the internet. It is particularly sad that in the current economic climate village shops and pubs are under threat of closure. If planning to call at a pub on route I suggest you contact it in advance to check its opening times and whether it serves food.

The Mawddach estuary

The small towns of Barmouth and Dolgellau are popular tourist destinations, and offer a good range of accommodation, shops, cafés, takeaways, pubs, banks etc. The nearest campsite to Barmouth is Hendre Mynach, ¾ mile north of Barmouth on the seaward side of the A496. The nearest campsite to Dolgellau is Tan-y-Fron, ½ mile east of the town centre.
On the southern side of the estuary, just off the trail is a campsite at Garthyfog, Arthog. There is B&B accommodation and camping at Graig Wen signposted from the Mawddach Trail just after the concrete tank traps. The main trail passes Kings youth hostel. Nearby is Hafod Dywyll

campsite. Routes A & C then pass Caban Cader Idris bunkhouse further down the Gwynant valley, and later the George III inn at Penmaenpool, offering accommodation food and drink. There is a bunkhouse at Cefn Coed, Ponderosa near Abergwynant Farm. Route B passes the Gwernan Hotel at Llyn Gwernan, whose bar and restaurant is open to non-residents *Thurs/Fri/Sat (12.00–15.00, 18.00–21.00)*.

On the northern side of the estuary there is B&B accommodation near the route at Trem Idris, Llanelltyd, Coed Cae, Taicynhaeaf, and further west at Borthwnog Hall. At Bontddu there is Tyddyn Du campsite.

Heading north from Barmouth to Llandecwyn

There are no facilities on the Ardudwy Way itself apart from a campsite on the route at Dinas. On the descent route to Llanbedr there is a camp site at Nantcol Waterfalls. In Llanbedr, which is the scheduled break point from the Ardudwy Way there is the Ty Mawr hotel and the Victoria Inn both providing accommodation and food. Additional B&B accommodation is available at Bryn Artro and Gwynfryn House. There are two stores and a butchers in the village.

Other small coastal communities linked to the trail also offer facilities and access to public transport. Tal-y-bont has a shop, inn, B&Bs, campsites, Italian restaurant and pizza takeaway. Dyffryn Ardudwy has two shops, an inn, B&Bs, hotel, café and campsite. Llanfair and nearby Llandanwg each has a B&B. Harlech has B&Bs, pubs, shops and eating options.

Where this section ends at Llandecwyn there are two adjoining B&Bs accessed from a driveway on the southern edge of the village beyond the war memorial: Awel-y-Mynydd (01766 770910) and Bryn Derw (01766 770345). There is also the option of following the minor road down from Bryn Bwbach to Talsarnau, where B&B is available at Estuary Cottage near the railway station.

Llandecwyn to Porthmadog

The trail passes through Maentwrog, where there is The Grapes Hotel, offering food and accommodation and Bryn Maen B&B. It continues to The Oakley Arms Hotel at Tan-y-bwlch, which offers food and accommodation. Also nearby Plas Tan-y-bwlch, the Snowdonia National Park Environmental

Centre offers individual dinner, B&B when a room is available, without requiring participation in any of its residential courses. There are no facilities then until you reach Penrhyndeudraeth, which has B&Bs, pubs, cafe, takeaways, Spar shop & Indian restaurant.

On the final section The trail passes Wenydd B&B at Minfordd, then Portmeirion, which offers various food and drink options during the day, as well as accommodation. Porthmadog is another popular tourist town offering B&Bs, shops, cafes, takeaways, pubs, banks etc

Heading south from Llandecwyn to Barmouth

There are no facilities on the first section to Harlech apart from a campsite near Ynys.

Harlech is another popular tourist centre, offering B&B, pubs, shops, ice cream parlour and eating options. The trail then passes Llanfair, which has a B&B, then descends to Llandanwg which has a B&B and a café by the beach car park. From Llanbedr station its is only ¼ mile into Llanbedr itself offering facilities previously described. The next section offers camping at Shell Island, then passes recommended Benar Beach campsite before reaching Tal-y-bont offering facilities previously described. On the final section to Barmouth the trail passes Trawsdir camp site, The Wayside pub, restaurant and fish bar midway, then Hendre Mynach campsite.

Tourist Information Centres

The following surviving Information Centre offers information and an accommodation booking service:

Harlech   01766 780658   tic.harlech@eryri-npa.gov.uk

www.visitmidwales.co.uk   www.visitsnowdonia.info

Train crossing Barmouth bridge

Transport

The Mawddach-Ardudwy Trail is supported by easily accessible public transport throughout most of its length, with local bus services and the Cambrian Coast Railway between Barmouth and Porthmadog. They offer good views and are an enjoyable part of the visiting experience.

The Mawddach estuary
The southern side of the Mawddach estuary is served by the 28 bus, Dolgellau to Tywyn, operated by Lloyds Coaches. The bus runs several times daily Monday – Saturday, except public holidays, with intermediate stops at Penmaenpool, Abergwynant on request, and Arthog. On Sunday the service is more limited.

The northern side of the estuary between Dolgellau and Barmouth is served by the X94 bus operated by Arriva. The bus runs hourly Monday -Saturday, except public holidays, with intermediate stops at Llanelltyd, Taicynhaeaf and Bontddu. On Sunday GHA operates a more limited X94 service.

Between Barmouth and Porthmadog
The coastal communities between Barmouth and Harlech are served by both bus and the Cambrian Coast Railway. Bus 38, operated by Express Motors, runs several times daily Monday – Saturday, excluding public holidays, with intermediate stops at Llanfair, Llanbedr, Dyffryn Ardudwy, Tal-y-bont,

Llanaber & Barmouth. Unfortunately, this bus no longer routinely extends to Llandecwyn, but check timetable for any reinstatement of this service. On Dolgellau college days there is currently a 1726 bus from Llandecwyn to Maentwrog and Tan-y-bwlch (Oakley Arms), and a 0730 bus back.

On Sundays only, bus no. 2, operated by Express Motors, runs twice during the morning from Tan-y-bwlch (Oakley Arms) to Llandecwyn and on to Harlech and Barmouth. In the other direction the no. 2 runs once during the morning and midday between Barmouth & Tan-y-bwlch (Oakley Arms).

Bus 1B, operated by Express Motors, runs hourly during the day Monday-Saturday between Porthmadog and Blaenau Ffestiniog, with intermediate stops at Minffordd, Penrhyndeudraeth, and Tan-y-bwlch (Oakley Arms).

The Cambrian Coast Railway operates an hourly service during the day between Pwllheli-Machynlleth-Birmingham, calling at Barmouth, Llanaber*, Tal-y-bont*, Dyffryn Ardudwy*, Llanbedr*, Pensarn*, Llandanwg*, Harlech, Tygwyn*, Talsarnau*, Llandecwyn*, Penrhyndeudraeth, Minffordd and Porthmadog. (* indicates a request stop at an unmanned station.) The railway is the key transport to and from Llandecwyn, especially if local accommodation is not available.

Public transport enquiries

www.gwynedd.gov.uk for bus & train timetables (transport & streets > public transport > timetables)

Arriva	0871 200 22 33
GHA	01978 753 598
Express Motors	01286 881108
traveline	0871 200 2233
National Rail	08457 484950
National Express	08705 8080